Solution Building in
Couples Therapy

Elliott Connie, MA, LPC, is a solution-focused therapist and trainer who works as a psychotherapist in his private practice in Keller, Texas. He specializes in using a solution-focused approach to work with couples and families. Additionally, he founded and oversees the Solution-Focused Training Institute, which holds multiple training sessions on this approach, including an annual symposium, workshops, and business consultations. He is the co-editor of the book *The Art of Solution Focused Therapy*. Connie has traveled throughout the United States and Europe, including the United Kingdom, Sweden, and Canada, conducting trainings and workshops to help professionals more effectively work with couples and to build more satisfying relationships in their lives. He is known for delivering interactive workshops and dynamic speeches that are focused on having an immediate impact on attendees' personal and professional lives. His humor and story-telling skills make him a highly sought-after lecturer and conference presenter.

Solution Building in Couples Therapy

Elliott Connie, MA, LPC

SPRINGER PUBLISHING COMPANY
NEW YORK

Springer Publishing Company, LLC
11 West 42nd Street
New York, NY 10036
www.springerpub.com

Acquisitions Editor: Nancy Hale
Composition: diacriTech

ISBN: 978-0-8261-0959-0
E-book ISBN: 978-0-8261-0960-6

12 13 14 15/ 5 4 3 2 1

The author and the publisher of this Work have made every effort to use sources believed to be reliable to provide information that is accurate and compatible with the standards generally accepted at the time of publication. The author and publisher shall not be liable for any special, consequential, or exemplary damages resulting, in whole or in part, from the readers' use of, or reliance on, the information contained in this book. The publisher has no responsibility for the persistence or accuracy of URLs for external or third-party Internet websites referred to in this publication and does not guarantee that any content on such websites is, or will remain, accurate or appropriate.

Library of Congress Cataloging-in-Publication Data

CIP data is available from the Library of Congress.

Special discounts on bulk quantities of our books are available to corporations, professional associations, pharmaceutical companies, health care organizations, and other qualifying groups. If you are interested in a custom book, including chapters from more than one of our titles, we can provide that service as well.

For details, please contact:
Special Sales Department, Springer Publishing Company, LLC
11 West 42nd Street, 15th Floor, New York, NY 10036-8002s
Phone: 877-687-7476 or 212-431-4370; Fax: 212-941-7842
Email: sales@springerpub.com

Printed in the United States of America by Gasch Printing.

To:
Geoffrey and Jeanette Connie for being the
relationship that created me.
Steve and Marie Crandall for being the relationship
that taught me.
Carmesia McJunkin-Connie for creating
a relationship with me.
Last but not least, to all of the couples that allowed me
to sit in the presence of their love throughout
the years, thank you!

Contents

Foreword

Elliott Connie has written a remarkable book. Read it and you will be taken on a journey. If you are new to the world of solution-focused therapy, beware! This book could capture your heart. And if you are an old hand, seen it, done it, and worn out the t-shirt, this book is the ticket to your second honeymoon.

As Elliott says from the very beginning, solution-focused therapy is simple, so simple it is really hard to learn. And from this book, if you set out to do so, you could teach yourself how to become a competent solution-focused therapist. It is all here, laid out clearly, packed with examples from the real world of therapy, repeated and repeated like onion skins, each repetition releasing its own flavor, a variation on a theme, and a new understanding of something already known.

How does Elliott do it? Breathe new life into an old onion? Because he takes us all on a journey in which we see the solution-focused world through *his* eyes. He does not guide us through his considerable knowledge and experience, but rather takes us on *his* voyage of discovery and through Elliott's eyes even the most familiar sights are no longer what were expected. Each solution-focused technique is discovered, brought to light, polished, and then practiced, sometimes with consummate skill and sometimes with the clumsy good luck of the beginner—Elliott does not make himself special. He saves that for the model he uses and for the clients represented in this book.

These clients appear and reappear in each chapter, the first time, understandably, in the Introduction where Elliott describes his first meeting with his first couple: "When the couple left my office, I still wasn't sure what had happened, but I was certain I loved it!" Elliott's work is full of this love: love for his clients and love of his model. In the Overview, Elliott meets the couple that brings him down to size and from whom he learns a skill, so obvious it is hard to believe how difficult it is. It comes from the question, "How did you two meet?," which Elliott has so often made one of the centerpieces of his work, and to amazing effect. Chapter by chapter, Elliott's clients return to illustrate each step of the solution-focused model while Elliott marvels at what they are teaching him. The lessons are vivid as well as clear and instructive, and between them Elliott inserts amusing or poignant stories from his own life, which always end by throwing a good light on the lives of his clients.

Pity that this book will be hard to find on any reading lists other than those engaged in work with couples. Yet, this is where it should be and where it should be in the top set. It is a book to engage in, to learn about, and learn to do solution-focused therapy, not only with couples but with anyone. Fortunately, all indications are that Elliott's voyage of discovery is only just beginning, and therefore we can expect more installments; more of the excitement and pleasure of his discoveries in future books.

Chris Iveson, MA
Therapist and Author
Co-Founder of BRIEF, London, UK

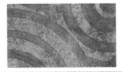

Foreword

As a marriage and family therapist for over 20 years, I must admit that I rarely smiled when I saw a couple scheduled on my therapy calendar. I enjoy helping families heal, but couples were a challenge. They always waited too long to come to therapy. They argued, bickered, fussed, and yelled at each other. They claimed that they either did not love each other anymore or could not decide whether they wanted to be married or not. They wanted me to decide their fate. Trying to help them was hard work as a solution-focused therapist, which equipped me with the belief that my clients were competent. The exceptions were there, I knew, but my clients often refused to acknowledge them. Until now. Elliott Connie has written a book that is word for word, a prescription for hope and a vehicle for couples to get back on track with their relationship and their lives. This book helps exceptions to surface in your office in a way that surprises them and invigorates their relationship. Solution building is magical to watch and feels magical to do.

This book also reminds those of us who have been married a long time to remember the good times on a bad day. Elliott has found a way through his solution-building process for couples to remember what caused each of the partners to notice each other in the first place which leads to a rekindling of lost feelings and emotions. When Elliott shared the questions in this book with me, I felt a door open in my therapy room to the future, and watched my couples walk through it. And they didn't just walk through it; they danced and laughed through it with new eyes and a reverence for their relationship that they had left on the side of the road when life interfered. I watched happily, as couples put aside blame and threats and embraced their preferred past, as Elliott writes in this book. I saw tearful, sad, and hopeless faces transform into shy smiles and glances at each other. I saw them put down their defenses and see each other as if for the first time, again.

This book will take you through a dramatically new way of helping couples reunite their lives no matter what the circumstances are that bring them to your office. It will confirm how maintaining a simple approach of inquiring how couples wish their best day to be will help them build a list of assets, resources, and competencies that will follow them home. This book will help you help couples save their relationships and bring you joy because you were there to watch.

But here is a word of caution: You won't make a lot of money by putting solution building to work in your practice . . . at least, not initially. The couples you will work with may not need you after two or three sessions. They will state to you with smiles and hand holding that there is really nothing more they need to talk about. They may make out and embarrass you, as Elliott's couple did in his waiting room. (Yes, it's that kind of book!) Divorce attorneys may stop buying you lunch. But then, never fear, because the couples you help will have friends who will call and make an appointment with you, and those friends will tell other friends. You will be known as the marriage counselor who has a different style, who talks differently. And soon, your practice will be as busy as Elliott's. Yet at the end of the day, you may leave your office with a smile on your face, just like the couples you worked with and you may even remark to yourself what I have started to remark to myself . . . "I like working with couples . . . in fact, they are my favorite clients."

Linda Metcalf, PhD, LPC, LMFT
Author and President of the American
Association for Marriage and Family Therapists

Acknowledgments

Before I say anything else, I first must acknowledge God. If not for Your guidance and care in my life none of this would have been possible. Also, I am deeply thankful to Jennifer Perillo, former Acquisitions Editor at Springer Publishing Company, for seeing the potential of this book, and to Nancy Hale for understanding how much this project meant to me. I appreciate your patience and communication with me throughout these many months.

I have been inspired by so many in the years it has taken me to write this book. My journey toward the solution-focused perspective began years ago when I met Linda Metcalf for the very first time. At that time I was introduced to the work of Steve de Shazer and Insoo Kim Berg. I knew immediately I would never be the same. Thank you so much for being so supportive and encouraging throughout the years.

Eventually, my journey and search for further learning took me to London, England, where I met Chris Iveson, Harvey Ratner, and Evan George. Sitting in their training room I once again knew that I was being exposed to something that would impact me deeply and forever impact the way I did my work with clients. Their mentorship and friendship continue to mean the world to me. Please consider this book as a salute to these three great men.

Along this journey I have been able to develop friendships with some great friends, in addition to the people mentioned above, that have talked to me and supported me through the process of generating ideas. I have spent hours walking along the streets of Malmo, Sweden, and London, England, sitting in hotel lobbies talking about different aspects of solution-focused ideas. Adam Froerer, Sara Smock, and Rayya Ghul, thank you for allowing me to call you my friends. I hope this book makes you proud and inspires you all to chase your dreams.

There are a few other people that I have to mention. If not for them this book would never have been written. Rebekka Ouer, thank you so much for your friendship; I love that we get to spend so much time talking about our work with clients. Keep searching! To Jessica Sheppard, you are the best! Period! This book would not have been accomplished if you had not been working at my side supporting me along the way. I can't wait to see what else we can do!

To my loving wife. You are the best thing that has ever happened to me. I have not always been the best husband but every day of our lives together I have pursued the best future we could have. Your support in my endeavors means so much to me and it is because of your love that I am truly living a DREAM!

Introduction

*"Imagining myself enjoying new cheese, even before I find it,
leads me to it."*

—Dr. Spencer Johnson

The idea for this book began shortly after I accepted my first job as a therapist. I was eager to finally have my own office, business cards, and the other trappings of the position. I was working at an agency that catered to children and their families, and since I'd completed my practicum in a similar agency, this new job seemed ideal for me. My enthusiasm proved to be short lived.

The new agency handled referrals by routing each call through an intake coordinator, who was responsible for deciding which therapist would be the best fit for new clients. On one of my first days at the agency, I received a referral that forever changed my use of solution-focused therapy on the certain kind of clients I'd be working with in the future.

I was excited to see that first referral sheet on my desk—until I noticed it was for a couple. "This must be a mistake," I thought. I had no desire to work with couples. One of the reasons I'd taken the job was because the agency specialized in children. This referral was all wrong for me. I begged the intake coordinator to assign the couple to another therapist. She informed me the couple had requested a male counselor, and because I was the only male on the payroll, I was it. Not wanting to seem difficult or jeopardize my new job, I returned to my office where I could panic in peace.

I just did not feel comfortable with the idea of working with couples. My master's program had prepared me well, but I'd completed my practicum working with adolescents and their families. I felt completely unprepared to deal with a couple. I started thinking of ways I could refer this couple out of the agency, but because we provided therapy at no charge to the clients, my options were limited. I didn't want my new employer thinking that I was incompetent or that I couldn't handle anything that came my way, so I began giving myself pep talks. I'd worked with individuals and groups, how different could this be? I tried to block out the horror stories I'd heard from other therapists about working with couples. In the end, I resigned myself to my fate. I called the couple and scheduled an appointment.

The days leading up to the appointment seemed like a countdown. Simply put, I was dreading the session. As the day drew nearer, I decided to do everything I could to ensure I'd be at my best. I met with the professor who'd introduced me to solution-focused therapy and shared my concerns with her. She was helpful, as always, but she confided that she, too, had trepidations about working with couples. I came to the conclusion that my only remaining hope was to read up on the subject. I figured there must be a wealth of books and journal articles about using solution-focused techniques in couples therapy. Of course, that wasn't the case. I was able to locate a few articles, but the mountain of information I was hoping for just wasn't there. I told my mentor, "Someone should write a book devoted solely about solution-focused therapy with couples." "Maybe it will be you," she said. At the time, I couldn't have imagined her being more wrong. But what happened when I finally saw that first couple is what put me on the path to writing this book.

When they arrived for the session, I vowed to put aside my apprehensions and concentrate on being helpful, but what I saw when I walked out to the lobby brought back my feelings of dread. There was a couple in their mid-thirties, seated on opposite sides of the waiting room, each with the unmistakable look of anger on their faces. As I walked them back to my office, not one word was spoken between them. As they sat down, the husband volunteered what had led them to seek counseling. His wife was involved with another man. He felt he could no longer trust her, and he wanted access to her email accounts as a way of keeping tabs on her. He was visibly angry. The wife was equally upset. She explained why she'd done what she had, and why she believed she deserved to keep her email passwords a secret from her husband. I have no idea why I said what I said next—perhaps I was so unsettled by the conversation I didn't know what else to say. I wasn't doing the things I normally do in sessions. We were already 15 minutes in, and I hadn't asked what I consider the most important question in solution-focused therapy, "What do you hope to accomplish here?" I felt I'd lost control of the session and wasn't being of any help. Then I asked, "How did you two meet?"

The couple's response shocked me. The mood in the room changed instantly. Smiling, the husband said, "Do you want to tell him or should I?" That caused them both to laugh out loud—and my jaw to drop. I wasn't sure what had happened, but in a matter of moments, they'd become a completely different couple. Although I was unclear about the reasons for it, I intended to take full advantage of the abrupt change.

I began to ask them solution-focused questions such as, "What do you hope we'll accomplish in our work together?," "How will you know we've accomplished something useful once you've left this office?," and, "What will you notice your partner doing?" The answers I got were fruitful, descriptive, and hopeful. As the husband and wife took turns answering—often describing their partner in glowing terms—I realized this was the first time in quite some time either of them had heard anything positive coming from the other. It was the first time since the incident that brought them to counseling that there seemed to be hope for their relationship. Toward the end of the session, I asked the wife what small thing she hoped her husband would do to further improve their relationship in the coming week. She said she wanted him to make the bed with her in it. This answer was so unexpected, I had to ask her to explain. She said she finds the sensation of fresh bed sheets wafting down on top of her to be sensual and relaxing, and that her husband hadn't done that for her in several years. Before I could ask the husband what small thing he hoped his wife would do for the relationship, he accepted his wife's assignment. "That's easy, I can do that." They then asked to schedule another session.

When the couple left my office, I still wasn't sure what had happened, but I was certain I loved it. I'd had so much fun working with this couple that I was actually looking forward to the next session. But when the day arrived, I had second thoughts. I found myself wondering which couple would show up for the appointment—the smiling couple that had left my office or the angry couple I'd met in the waiting room. When the receptionist called to tell me my clients had arrived, I was review-ing my notes from the first session. When she called a second time, no more than 2 minutes later, to remind me that they were still waiting, I was a bit surprised by her anxious behavior. When she arrived in my office just a few minutes later to give me a third reminder, I was concerned that something might be wrong. Something was. When I got to the waiting room, my clients were engaged in rather a passionate public display of affection.

"Wow, they must have had a very different week," I thought. When I was finally able to get them apart and into my office, I almost couldn't believe what I heard them saying. Each partner had had a wonderful week and both believed this would be their last session. I asked what had changed. The husband said he felt he could trust his wife again. She said she felt loved again. All I could think was, how could this have happened in a week? I asked them how they'd managed to make those changes. The husband said that on the very next morning following our session, he'd dropped the bed sheets on his wife several times before he went to work. When he got home that evening, he found that his wife was out, but had left him a note. She apologized for what she'd done and listed all her email passwords. The husband then logged on to her computer and read her communications. The wife had emailed the other man that morning after the husband had left for work. She wrote that she'd had a change of heart—she now felt her marriage was worth saving and that she and the other man could no longer see each other.

I listened as the couple went on to describe a week in which they went back to concentrating on one another and doing the things that had made their relationship work well in the past. Toward the end of the session, they expressed their belief that this positive behavior would continue, and true to their prediction, no further sessions were scheduled.

In the following weeks and months, I often thought about that couple and wondered if what I'd witnessed in my office would actually endure. It wasn't that I lacked confidence in the solution-focused approach or doubted this therapy could be successfully applied to couples, it was just that it had all seemed too easy in this case. When I mentioned the couple to my peers at the agency—none of whom were experienced with solution-focused techniques—they were universally of the opinion that the couple had decided to seek counseling elsewhere and had merely declined to tell me so to my face. I might have agreed with them if it were not for a Christmas card I received several months later. The couple reported they were still together and still doing well.

This experience had been so enjoyable for me that I asked the agency's intake coordinator to send more couples my way. I was hooked. I couldn't remember what it was about couples that made me so nervous in the beginning. As the years went on, I left that agency and began working with couples in private practice, gaining more and more confidence and developing ways of applying solution-focused therapy (SFT) that worked for me. From the moment I first heard of it, SFT had made sense to me, but it took time for me to trust it and become comfortable using it. I was applying SFT with a patient population that many practitioners regard as stressful or even refuse to see in their practices—and I was having fun doing it. When a colleague at a local university heard that I had a practice that catered to couples, he invited me to conduct a training session for his staff and students. It was the first time I fully realized the extent to which many clinicians feel apprehensive about the idea of working with couples. Since then, it's been my goal to help therapists overcome such feelings and to become comfortable and competent with relationship therapy. At a workshop in Sweden, one of the attendees suggested I consider writing a book on the subject because there was so little available literature. Recalling the difficulty I'd had in finding resources before I saw my first couple, I certainly recognized the problem.

This book is about the process of conducting solution-focused conversations with couples. The information here is not meant to be a "how to" manual. Instead, I'm simply offering examples of ways I've used the approach in my clinical work with couples, and drawing on foundational information about solution-focused tenets that were originally developed by Steve de Shazer and Insoo Kim Berg (De Jong & Berg, 2008).

Working with couples presents a unique set of challenges, and this book sets forth a way of working through those challenges using solution-focused methods. I purposely say *a* way rather than *the* way because I certainly do not believe this is the only way. It's simply the way that works for me.

I've learned from some extraordinary teachers, including Linda Metcalf, Chris Iveson, Harvey, Ratner, and Evan George, all of whom took time to mentor me, and I've learned much from the writings of Steve de Shazer, Insoo Kim Berg, Yvonne Dolan, Brian Cade, and Alastair MacDonald. Still, my most important teachers over the years have been my clients. The couples I've seen have taught me the kind of questions they find helpful and demonstrated the power of having hopeful conversations.

In anticipation of writing this book, I gave a great deal of thought about how to organize it in a way that would be most helpful to readers. Because I've developed a process I've used in working with couples, it seemed logical to devote a chapter of the book to a detailed explanation of each step in the process. Because I also wanted to use actual case histories to illuminate the process, much of this book is the case study of one real couple, drawn from transcripts of my sessions with them. I've changed their names and the details of their lives to protect their privacy, but the outcome is real.

A colleague of mine once told me that in order to truly become effective at solution-focused therapy, students must read about it, see it in action, and experience it for themselves. By including actual case studies along with common solution-focused questions, exercises, and hopeful stories, I hope that interested readers can practice as they read.

When I conduct workshops, it's always my goal to give attendees something they can use in their work on the very next day. My goal here is the same. I hope that by the end of this book, you will have learned something that will make a difference in your work, something that will increase your confidence and reduce the frustration that sometimes comes in working with couples.

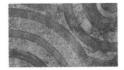

An Overview of Solution-Focused Therapy

"Man's mind stretched to a new idea never goes back to its original dimensions."
—OLIVER WENDELL HOLMES, JR.

Working with couples in solution-focused therapy (SFT) is little different from working with individuals on the same basis. The process is the same—namely, an emphasis on the client's preferred future as opposed to the problem that led to therapy. What differs is the construction of the conversation. Conducting conversations based on client desires, strengths, and resources with two people involved in a romantic relationship can sometimes be challenging. How can you have a conversation about desires, strengths, and resources if one of the two parties feels hurt or has no interest in participating? Addressing this challenge is one of the reasons for writing this book. SFT with couples requires the therapist to keep the discussion targeted squarely on solutions—and to avoid any distractions related to the couple's problem story.

The information in this chapter includes a brief review of the guiding tenets of SFT. Whether you are new to solution-focused (SF) ideas or an expert in this field, reviewing the basics before exploring applications in couple's therapy is appropriate.

SOLUTION-FOCUSED TENETS

SFT was developed by Steve de Shazer and Insoo Kim Berg at the Brief Family Therapy Center in Milwaukee (de Shazer et al., 2007). Their approach built on the work of the Mental Research Institute (MRI) in Palo Alto, California, which in turn drew on Wittgensteinian philosophy and Buddhist principles (de Shazer et al., 2007). As outlined in the book, *More than Miracles: The State of the Art of Solution-Focused Brief Therapy*, an SF practice adheres to the key tenets that follow.

If It Ain't Broke, Don't Fix It

If the client does not report something to be a problem, or if they describe a problem they've solved, no further intervention is required. This may seem basic, even obvious, but there are therapeutic approaches that don't follow this principle. When I was new to SFT, I was working at a community mental health center providing in-home family therapy. One of the requirements of the job was participating in weekly clinical supervision meetings with the team of practitioners and supervisors. My colleagues in the group practiced traditional, problem-focused approaches to therapy, and often questioned my SF methods. A frequent topic in our staff meetings was the idea of seeing clients for "maintenance," or developing strategies that would facilitate the client "growth." Although these are appropriate ideas from a problem-focused perspective, the thought that clients need to continue therapy for maintenance and growth is totally incongruent with SFT.

If It Works, Do More of It

One of the ideas that most appeals to me about SFT is the presumption that everyone is doing something well in their lives. This simple belief communicates hope, respect, and optimism to the client. It is rooted in the idea that no matter how serious a problem may be or how long the client has struggled with it, there must be something that person is doing well in their lives, some inherent trait that can be brought to bear to accomplish a positive change. Some years ago, I was conducting a group for parents of children involved in the local county's drug program. On the first night of the program, the group members introduced themselves, offering information about their occupations and details of their family. One mother identified herself as a local high school teacher who worked with the school's most difficult children. She said that she was in the group because her own children did not follow her rules at home, and she was clearly upset by it. When another parent asked how a mother was able to get the kids in her classroom to listen to her, the mother's demeanor changed immediately. She explained the system that she used in her classroom and how effective it was for her. Several of the other parents began taking notes, believing clearly that this woman was the one who knew how to motivate teens, but she simply forgot to take those skills home with her. By the end of the meeting, the mother had created a plan to use her classroom skills at home with her own kids. She'd come to the group stressed and frustrated, but she'd also come carrying the solution. She just didn't realize it. In identifying for herself the things she does well and giving herself permission to do more of those things, she was able to develop an effective solution to a problem she'd been struggling with for sometime.

If It's Not Working, Do Something Different

Please note the word *different*, not *better*. This is an important distinction to understand this tenet of SFT. A common misconception of this approach is that it is *problem solving*. On the contrary, it is *solution building*, and a solution is only a solution if it works (de Shazer et al., 2007). This may seem obvious, but many people repeat the behaviors that don't work simply because it's the way they were taught or the way they've always done things. This tenet asks the therapist to consider efficacy. If a task is not effective then there's no reason to continue with it. Other options should be explored.

This idea is very different from the thinking of practitioners who operate from other theoretical perspectives. For example, in my clinical staff meetings at the community center, one of the regular procedures was reviewing interventions that had been developed by the therapists for their clients' families. Each therapist would present a case summary and outline tasks developed in the previous sessions. It was common that the group would offer feedback to the presenting therapist without considering the most important question: Did the intervention work? There seemed to be more concern into how "creative" the intervention was or how "right" it seemed. But from the SF perspective, if the intervention is not effective then it should be discontinued. It's just that simple.

Small Steps Can Lead to Big Changes

It is widely accepted that problems can snowball, that is, they can start off small and grow bigger with time. Solutions can behave in the same way, although that fact is not as widely accepted. This is what makes practicing SFT so rewarding for me. More often than not, people come into therapy with a problem they've been wrestling with for a long time. They come with a hope—but not often with the belief—that the problem will be overcome. If at the end of the session, often the first session, a simple task is given to make things slightly better then the confidence can be built. An emphasis on moving slowly in simple steps makes a future resolution seem more achievable. The growth of hope is a common result.

Solution Is Not Necessarily Directly Related to the Problem

While working at the community center, one of my supervisors insisted that for a therapist's intervention to be effective, it must be directly related to the problem, and therefore, a thorough examination of the problem is required. SFT takes a different view—and very little or no time is spent exploring the problem (de Shazer et al., 2007). SFT tosses the traditional problem/solution approach out the window and begins by identifying how the clients' lives would look without the problem (de Shazer et al., 2007). Once this has been established, a plan to create a life without the problem can be developed using the client's own skills and resources. More often than not, the solutions developed aren't directly related to the problem.

Once I worked with a business woman who was experiencing tremendous stress at work. She was a high-ranking executive who had previously enjoyed her job, but was now dealing with a new boss and having a hard time with new demands that were suddenly being placed on her. Thinking about her situation from the perspective of my former supervisor, a solution might have been developed that was related directly to her work or her relationship with the new boss. Instead, after a careful examination of how her life would look without a problem, a potential solution became clear.

She used her own skills and past successes to develop a strategy that proved to be quite effective for her, yet was not directly related to her job situation. Instead of focusing on somehow fixing the relationship she had with her boss she decided to focus on her family. She began to take time each night to spend time with her kids and husband. Often times as few as 15 minutes, and make sure she shared a few moments of what she called, "smiles." Almost immediately this simple strategy allowed her to enjoy her job.

The Language of Solution Development Is Different From the Language of Problem Description

SF practice differs from other therapeutic approaches in its use of solution building rather than problem solving. The language of solution building is positive and forward-looking, whereas the language of problem solving is negative and backward-looking (George, Iveson, & Ratner, 2006). Rather than delving into the past problem, SFT asks that the clients look ahead to what their lives will be like when the problem is behind them—instead of sitting in traffic cursing the roadblock ahead, visualize the open road that lays beyond it.

SOLUTION BUILDING WITH COUPLES

Understanding what it means to build solutions and how to use the solution-building language is crucial in using SFT with couples. The differences between solution building and problem solving can be subtle, but they have a significant impact on the therapeutic conversation. Keeping conversations centered on solutions is challenging with couples, but it is the clinician's responsibility to ask questions that keep the conversation from dissolving into problem talk. Problem talk leads to sessions spent arguing, debating, and yelling—all of the negatives that led the couple to seek help in the first place. By spending time building solutions, the therapist can both keep the conversation moving in a productive manner and avoid time spent defusing arguments.

In the book *Interviewing for Solutions*, Peter Dejong and Insoo Kim Berg (2002) define the over-arching ideas of solution building. Here, I'd like to focus on solution building as a conversation, and on the tools required to have such a conversation with couples. SF questions are designed to help couples do just three things: (1) identify a preferred future; (2) shift from a problem orientation to a solution orientation; and (3) identify the steps that are required to create the identified preferred future. That's the simplicity of SFT.

The solution-building process is about creating what is most desired by the couple, and not about problem solving. Repeatedly, couples come into therapy not agreeing on the origins of the problem that led them there. This makes problem solving difficult—the first task becomes getting both of them on the same page about the problem. Even if a couple can agree that they are coming to therapy because, for example, one of the partners has been discovered to be having an affair, they may never agree on the origins of the problem that led to the affair. Such debate can go on and on and lead nowhere. In contrast, I've noticed that when you ask a couple about their desires for the relationship, the conversation goes in a much different direction.

Couples often come to my office with the assumption that I'm going to be interested in the origins of their problem, and that my understanding of the origins will be essential in helping them. This may lead one or both of the partners to want to explain the problem from their individual perspective. As I write this, I cannot think of a single instance of a couple recounting their problem story to me with any unanimity. In fact, the perspectives are so drastically divergent that I find myself wondering whether the two parties are in the same relationship. Couples who assume that I will be interested in their problem story are often surprised to learn that I'm interested in something entirely different—I ask questions about the things they want to happen in their relationship in the future without the problem they're facing now. Interestingly, the answers I hear always fall into one of two categories. The first is an answer that's exactly the same for both parties. Although they may have been in complete disagreement about the origin of their problem, they are in complete agreement about their hopes for the future: both express the desire for a loving relationship, more intimacy, and so on. The second kind of

6

answer involves hopes for the future that are expressed differently by the partners, but are agreeable to both. For example, one person might say, "I wish there could be more intimacy and better communication in our future relationship." Although this may not be exactly what the other partner is hoping for, he or she will nonetheless express a willingness to work toward it. At times, both the partners will list things they are hoping for, which are also agreeable to the other partner. The process of discovering what the couple collectively wants allows solution building to begin. That's all solution building is—using the client's language to identify the "details of a preferred future, and building a world that includes those details." Although it is simple to express, the process is hard to execute. It requires a special set of skills to prevent the problem talk from interrupting solution building, and it requires the practitioners to be courageous enough to ask questions they are curious about, but wise enough to know the difference between what is their business and what is not.

First Principles

As we've seen, the SF process is simple. However, there is difficulty in understanding the difference between information that is our business, which requires the therapist to be curious, and information that is not our business, which requires the therapist to remain silent. That takes discipline and focus. What follows are the principles a therapist can keep in mind to increase discipline and focus.

Every Couple Comes From a Successful Past

For a couple to be seeking therapy together, there has to have been a time in the past when the relationship was working better for both the parties. Yet, many couples come to therapy unaware that they've had a successful past and are unprepared to discuss it. It's common for new clients to think, "We've always had this problem" or "He or she has always been this way," but that's not the whole truth. For a relationship to have lasted any length of time, it cannot be the whole truth. There simply must be more to the story. The successful part of the relationship must be lying dormant. An important goal of SFT with couples is to awaken dormant successes so that they can play a role in the current relationship.

Connect With the Couple, Not Just the Individuals Within the Couple

This simple step can be accomplished in a number of ways. As in individual therapy, it is important that rapport be built between the therapist and the clients, but accomplishing this with two people requires the therapist to have a different set of skills and to ask different questions. By focusing on the relationship and the skills that each partner uses to contribute to the relationship, the therapist conveys a level of hope to the couple. This can be accomplished by simply getting to know the couple *as a couple*—by asking questions about lives, dreams, and accomplishments *together*.

Direct Each Question to Both Members of the Couple

I think of this rule as SF tennis. One day, while watching myself conduct a therapy session with a couple on a video tape, I noticed my head was moving back and forth as if I was watching a tennis match. That's because each question I asked about the details of the desired future was posed, in turn, to each partner. It is important that both members of the couple be allowed to express their ideas and thoughts throughout the session and to contribute equally to the building of the solution. To be clear, when I say both partners should contribute equally, I don't mean that each person needs to get equal time in the conversation. SF tennis simply means each person gets to take an equal number of turns in the conversation. Whether the turn lasts only a matter of seconds or goes on for several minutes, the fact that each partner took a turn allows each partner to contribute.

The Beauty Is in the Details So Focus on Them

Many years ago, when taking a driver's education course in high school, I learned an important lesson about details and perspective. I was taught to drive in a car equipped with a second set of brakes on the passenger side for the instructor to use in emergencies. My instructor had a habit of aggressively applying those brakes anytime she noticed that my eyes were not looking straight ahead. I found this quite annoying and eventually I got up my nerve to complain. The instructor explained that she hit the brakes whenever my eyes were not looking forward because a car

8

tends to drift in the direction of the driver's eyes. According to her, that's because the hands also tend to follow the direction of the eyes. Something similar happens in SF therapy. When partners of a couple have a detailed conversation about their past successes or their desires for the future, their lives tend to steer toward the details.

Early in my career, I got a call from a young woman who was looking to get into therapy with her husband. She didn't mention the reason for her seeking help, but I knew the issue was serious because she asked for a session as soon as possible, and because I could hear her husband yelling at her in the background throughout the call. When they arrived for their first session a few days later, it was clear that the two were upset with each other. Similar to the very first couple I worked with, I found these partners sitting on separate couches in my lobby. When I invited them into my office, I saw them exchanging dirty looks as they got up. I knew I was in for a long hour. Without a smile or any other show of affection, they sat down in my office—again on separate couches. We spent the first few minutes trying to establish best hopes for the therapy (George, Iveson, & Ratner, 2006), but I could sense the conversation growing more and more tense. Then I remembered to ask the questions that had been so effective with my first couple, "How did you two meet?" It worked like a charm. The couple recalled how they'd met at a business party, and as each additional detail of their meeting and early relationship came out, the couple grew closer and closer right there in front of me. Throughout the conversation, they treated each other with respect and kindness, and at the end of the session, they walked out holding hands.

They weren't the same couple I'd met in my lobby, and when they returned for the second session, it was clear the changes had been sustained. I began by asking what had been better for them, and they spent almost the entire hour detailing their progress over the past week. Toward the end of the session, I asked them how they were able to make these changes. The couple said they didn't recall many details of our first session. The part they did remember—which they gave full credit for all the changes—was the beginning, when they recalled the details of their meeting and early relationship. At least in part, my ego was damaged. I felt I had conducted a good session, but all the couple remembered was what they had done for themselves. It's a lesson I carry with me to this day. A detailed discussion about a couple's success may be all it takes to build the solution. This couple taught me that the more you can concentrate the conversation on the details of a couple's successes (past, present, or future), the more likely the couple will be to steer their lives in the direction of those details, just as a car steers in the direction of the driver's eyes.

Carefully Choose What Parts of the Couple's Story to Be Curious About

An important skill in learning to work with couples, and perhaps with individuals, as well, is being disciplined enough to know the difference between data the couple presents that should be attended to by the therapist and information that should not. This skill has taken me several years of conducting sessions to develop, and even now I wish I were better at. I wish I could clearly explain do what you need to do to be able to identify information that should be attended to and information that shouldn't, but it's not always clear and it varies from session to session. I can say it requires listening for facts that are related to the couple's best hopes and not getting sucked into the problem story. The way I explain it in workshops is to say that therapists are like taxi drivers. The first task is to ask where they are going and to elicit a detailed description of that destination. It requires discipline not to suggest other destinations and not get distracted by the side roads that become available along the way. The whole of the work needs to be related to the chosen destination and nothing else. With time and practice, the therapist's ability to listen only for relevant information and to build questions using the client's own language will steer the taxi toward the couple's desired destination—and nowhere else.

Co-Construction Requires Using the Couple's Language

I first studied SFT with Evan George, Chris Iveson, and Harvey Ratner at BRIEF in London, and much of the training was about developing questions when working with couples. They taught that a therapist should use the same language the client uses in their answer to ask the next question. It is a profound idea, and I immediately began applying it in my work with couples. The process of co-construction requires that each person's language be attended to in great detail and used to build all the questions that follow. For example:

Therapist: What are your best hopes for therapy?

Husband: We just don't want to be fighting anymore.

Wife: Yeah, the fighting is ruining our relationship, and I am not sure how much longer I can take it.

Therapist: If sometime in the near future the two of you figure out a way to stop the fighting, what do you suppose you would be doing rather than fighting that will work much better for you?

Husband: I suppose I would rather be getting along, like we used to.

Wife: It would be so nice to love again.

Therapist: So getting along and being more loving would work better for you. What would that look like in your relationship?

The above sequence was transcribed from a recent session and outlines the idea of co-constructing conversations with couples. Notice that a bit of each partner's response was used by the therapist to formulate the next question. By that means, each member of the couple contributes to the direction of the therapy, thereby increasing the therapeutic alliance.

HOW SFT IS DIFFERENT?

From my earliest exposure to SFT, I was curious about what makes this approach, and those who practice it, different. In fact, that was the subject of my first book, *The Art of Solution-Focused Therapy* (Connie & Metcalf, 2009). In that book, several practitioners reported on applying SF methods in different settings such as counseling, psychiatry, marriage, family therapy, and so on. The more I spend time attending trainings, working with clients, and reading about SFT, the more I have come to believe that there are several additional keys that are effective in using this approach with couples.

It Is So Simple, It Is Almost Complicated

This phrase may seem like an oxymoron, but the SF approach to counseling is so simple and basic that sticking to it can be a challenge. Steve de Shazer (1985) explained that the process of developing interventions should follow a principle known as Occam's Razor, which holds that, all other things being equal, the simplest solutions are best. This idea applies equally well to the other steps of solution building. Solution building is a process of minimalism and simplicity. Although many of us may have spent years in graduate school learning how to identify and assess problems, and how to solve them using various counseling techniques, the only skill the SF therapist needs to build solutions is the ability to ask the next question.

Solution Building Is Based on Turn-Taking

Solution-building conversations must be co-constructed with input from all participants. To ensure that the conversation is *equally* co-constructed, each person involved must contribute to it equally. This can be a challenge with couples since it means that three people will be taking turns. To visualize this idea in a couple's therapy session, imagine that each partner has a paint brush that's been dipped into a color, red for one partner and blue for the other. Each time a partner answers a question, they put a stroke of paint on a canvas—the longer the response, the longer the stroke. At the end of the session, there should be an equal number of red and blue strokes. The strokes will be of unequal length, and it's possible that one color will dominate, but the number of red and blue strokes should be the same. That can happen only if each partner gets a turn to answer every question posed by the therapist.

Every Couple Is Motivated by Something

Motivation should never be in doubt, even if one member of the couple claims that he or she is only there because the other partner "made" them come to therapy. The idea of resistance to therapy has simply never made sense to me. How can I consider anyone who has sought out therapy (even if mandated), scheduled an appointment, and followed through by attending the session, to be resistant? I once heard Chris Iveson say that one of the things that he enjoys most about practicing SFT is that all of his clients are motivated. In watching Iveson's practice, it was clear to me that he treats each of his clients as if their motivation was not a question— no matter what it is. Making this presumption is crucial in conducting solution-building conversations with couples. The simple fact that the couple makes it into your office suggests that they were driven to do so by a desire for some form of change or a hope for some preferred outcome. When the therapist is able to make that change or preferred outcome part of the conversation, the couple's motivation becomes quite apparent— and grows as the conversation progresses.

SUMMARY

Working with couples from the SF perspective requires a shift from the idea that *problems must be solved* to *solutions must be built*. This shift is what this book is all about. Making this shift is difficult, because it requires therapists to adhere closely to a simple process that, at times, goes against their nature or even their training as clinicians. For me, learning the SF approach meant I had to unlearn processes associated with other approaches. I found it a challenging but worthwhile process. The truth is that when I was first exposed to SFT and subsequently began applying it in couple's therapy, I had some doubts. The ideas made perfect sense to me but I couldn't help thinking, "It can't be that easy." I truly did not believe psychotherapy could be so simple. But my clients over the years have taught me that, although the work can be hard at times, the approach is indeed simple—and quite helpful for couples.

Step 1:
Establishing a Destination

"You'll be surprised to know how far you can go from the point you thought was the end."

—UNKNOWN

Michelle and Stephanie are a lesbian couple who had been together for about 7 years when they came to see me. I could hear them arguing in my lobby, and when I walked out, I could see that they were upset with each other. When I invited them back to my office, they walked quietly. The following dialogue from that first session—following brief introductions—demonstrates how we worked together to establish a "best hope" for their therapy.

> Therapist: So, what are your best hopes for coming into my office today?
>
> Michelle: I don't know, just to work it out. Have some direction. Get some outside insight.
>
> Therapist: How would you know you were working it out in a way that was right for you?
>
> Michelle: I don't know.

Therapist: What do you think? What would give you a clue that you and Stephanie were working it out?

Michelle: We would be close again and communicating.

Therapist: That would be a sign that things were well, if you were close again and communicating? Stephanie, what about you, what are your best hopes for being here?

Stephanie: I guess I would like a change. That is how I would know something was different.

Therapist: What type of change?

Stephanie: Like uh . . .

Michelle: We are really going through some things.

Stephanie: Positive change. Like she said, communicating and doing things for each other, spending more time together. Um, I guess, desiring each other, stuff like that.

Therapist: So, if the two of you noticed those things happening, you would look back on these meetings as being helpful to you?

Michelle: Yes, definitely.

Stephanie: Yes.

The first time I heard the phrase *best hopes* was at a conference with Chris Iveson, Harvey Ratner, Evan George, and Guy Shennan at BRIEF in London. Iveson showed a videotape of a session with one of his clients demonstrating how he and his colleagues use solution-focused techniques. The very first question Iverson asked was, "What are your best hopes for this conversation?"

At the time, I had no idea I would become a student of these men and travel to their clinic every year, but the more time I spent with them over the years, watching their work and sharing my work with them, the more the best hopes question became a part of my working life.

Establishing a best hope for therapy is key to the therapeutic process because it establishes the direction for the rest of the conversation. This chapter reviews a number of questions a therapist can ask to

16

establish a best hope for each of their client couples. In their practice manual, George, Iveson, Ratner, and Shennan (2009) refer to the best hopes question as the "getting down to business" phase of the session. Beginning with this question allows therapists and their clients to begin building solutions early on.

AN EFFECTIVE BEST HOPE MUST . . .

Look Toward the Future

In the preceding dialogue, the therapist asked a series of questions relating to how things will be in the future. This is especially important to couples because details of the past may be painful or a source of disagreement between the partners. A helpful question would be, "How would you like tomorrow to look?" It's not unusual for the couples to be caught off guard and to answer such a question with "I don't know." The therapist must accept the answer and push on, using what the client says to build the next question. By asking something like, "How do you hope it would look?" the therapist allows the client to be heard but also keeps the conversation moving toward solutions.

Assume the Couple Wants to Be Together

One of the questions I'm frequently asked is how I handle the situation if one member of the couple does not want the relationship to continue. My answer is always the same—I never allow myself to believe that. It doesn't make sense for me to believe it—for two reasons. First, it makes my job of being helpful to the couple more difficult. Regardless of how one member of the couple may or may not feel, they've sought relationship counseling together. That means my role is to be as helpful to both of them as possible and to discover where the process of therapy will lead. To allow myself to believe that one of the parties no longer wants to be in the relationship only complicates the process unnecessarily. Second, the act of seeking marriage counseling is, by its very nature, an act of hope. The fact that both parties have come to a counselor's office says that both of them believe in the relationship on some level and have at least some hope that they can achieve higher levels of happiness. Getting a couple to realize that simple fact can often be an effective intervention in and of itself.

Leave the Past in the Past

Couples rarely agree on the problem that brings them to therapy, and spending time trying to reach agreement only slows down the therapeutic process. As de Shazer et al. (2007) point out, the problem is always negative and always involves discussion of the past. The task of a couples therapist in establishing best hopes is to have a positive conversation about the future. Negative conversations about the past are in direct conflict with that and should be avoided. That doesn't mean the therapist should ignore a client who brings up a past problem. Instead, the therapist should carefully choose a response that acknowledges the problem but moves the conversation toward a more positive discussion of the future.

Establish a Contract

This is an idea first introduced by Iveson, George, and Ratner at their London clinic. The best hopes question is described as establishing a *contract* with the client. It's the process of identifying a clearly stated desired future outcome that the clients can agree on and the therapist believes is achievable. This is an important step—perhaps the most important step—in therapy. It sets the direction for the rest of the work. It's particularly challenging in couples therapy because three people are involved. The best hopes answer of each partner in the relationship must match or be seen as mutually beneficial, so that both parties will be engaged in the process and be able to assist the other in their pursuit of the desired outcome.

THE THERAPIST'S TASK IN ESTABLISHING BEST HOPES

Think of establishing a best hope as selecting a destination rather than setting a goal. It may seem a subtle difference, but I believe *destination* more accurately depicts what we're seeking in this type of therapy. A solution-focused practitioner does something very different in sessions than those who practice more traditional forms of therapy, so the language describing what's being done should also be different. I've sat in many training sessions conducted by clinicians who work with couples, and they often talk about the pursuit of goals. The word always strikes me as wrong—it's not what I think I'm doing when I work with couples. Direction seems more useful and descriptive to me.

In establishing the direction of therapy with a couple, the therapist must be disciplined and stay on task until the proper best hopes have been identified, because that will be the basis for subsequent conversations. One of the most common errors made by new practitioners is moving the conversation forward before a well-defined direction has been established and agreed on. Notice that in the earlier dialogue, the therapist was careful to confirm with the clients that the direction under consideration would be useful to them. That signals to the couple that the therapist has heard what they are saying and demonstrates to them that the therapist will work to move the relationship in that direction.

Another task for the therapist at this point in the process is to reject any invitation to be drawn into problem talk. In the earlier conversation, one of the partners volunteered, "We are really going through some things." In more traditional forms of therapy, that might have been seen as an opening that should be further explored. Instead, the therapist continued to focus on establishing a direction for the future. Clients will often make problem statements because they believe it's information the therapist needs to know. However, when presented with this kind of information, the task for the solution-focused therapist is simple: attend carefully to information that looks forward—and leave the rest aside. Don't be curious about, or become drawn into, the couple's problem story.

LOST IN LONDON:
A PERSONAL STORY

My first trip to London for training at the brief therapy practice was also my first trip abroad, and my education began on the very afternoon I arrived. I was eager to see what I could of London before my appointment the next morning, so I set out on a walking tour of the city with my aunt, who was traveling with me. Feeling tired after our long flight, my aunt soon asked to return to the hotel. I handed her our only room key (mistake number one) and pushed on without her. I wandered about, taking in the sights for hours, listening to music on my cell phone as I walked, until I'd exhausted both myself and my cell phone's battery (mistake number two). Finally ready to head back, I turned in what I thought was the direction of my hotel, but nothing looked familiar. I walked on, hoping to spot a landmark that would put me on the right path, but the farther I walked, the clearer it became: I was hopelessly lost. A passerby suggested that I could ask a cab driver for help. It was a brilliant idea—London cabbies are legendary for their knowledge of the city. I quickly hailed a cab, but once inside, I realized to my horror that I didn't know the name of my hotel. When the driver asked, "Where to?" I could only answer, "I don't know." All I could recall was that my hotel was part of a major chain. The driver shut off the engine and turned to ask me, "What does your hotel look like?" He said if I could describe the destination in enough detail, he was sure he could find it. I immediately felt more relaxed. He asked specific questions about the location of the hotel. "How long did it take to get there from the air-port?" About 30 minutes. "Did you pass Buckingham Palace on the way?" Yes. "Did you cross the river?" No.

The questioning went on like that for about 10 minutes, and from my answers, the driver informed me he was certain of my hotel's gen-eral vicinity. "Now I just need to know what it looks like." It was at that point I realized that this discovery process was very much like a solution-focused therapy session. I was simply describing a destination, and the more details I was able to provide, the more hopeful I became that we'd actually get there. I told the driver what the front of the hotel, the lobby, and some of the surrounding buildings looked like. I was surprised at the level of detail I was able to recall. After another 10 minutes or so, the driver confidently announced, "You're at the Hilton." Only then did the driver put the cab in gear and head out into traffic. Thirty minutes later, I had safely returned to my room.

When I look back on this experience, I can only marvel at how lucky I was, how dumb I'd been, and how helpful the cabbie had man-aged to be. Despite his extraordinary willingness to help me, he might have unwittingly made matters worse by asking the wrong questions or driving around for hours trying to retrace my steps. Instead, he focused on the future, and it was the details of my desired destination that led us to it. I often recount this story in trainings because it illustrates something very important about establishing best hopes with clients. In addition to asking helpful questions, my driver did something equally important that night—he didn't move the cab until it was clear where we were going. This is a lesson I'd like every student of solution-focused therapy to learn: don't move on to other parts of the process until you and your clients have agreed on the desired destination.

ONE CHANCE TO HELP:
A CASE EXAMPLE

Not long ago my assistant received a rather odd phone call. A potential client had called wanting to set up a session with her husband. She asked if anything useful could be accomplished in a single session, since that was all her husband had agreed to attend. My assistant told her that although no promises could be made, she'd check with me to see if I was comfortable working under that kind of limitation. I agreed, and the appointment was scheduled.

When the couple arrived in my office, it was clear that the husband was unhappy to be there. When I asked, "What are your best hopes for therapy?" he said he had no hopes—he'd only agreed to come because his wife had insisted and he wanted to "shut her up." The wife said her hope was that she and her husband could move beyond their current problem. I asked her how she would know when they had accomplished that. She said her husband would move back into their home, they'd get back to communicating well, and there'd be more affection between them. I again asked the husband what his best hopes would be and he repeated that he didn't have any—but this time, he seemed less annoyed by the question. "Even though you're here for your wife," I asked him, "what would make this satisfying to you in some way?" He said he'd also like it if they could move past their problem, but that moving on is something that's difficult to him. He admitted to a history of not letting go of problems—when people in his life hurt him, he simply cut them off. He knew he couldn't do that with his wife, he said, but he didn't think he could put their problem behind him either. I then asked if he were somehow able to handle his current problem differently—without knowing exactly how just yet—how would his life be different? He said life would be more like the life his wife had described. The two of them would be living together again, communication would improve, and they would have a more affectionate relationship. Satisfied that a usable direction had been achieved, I moved the conversation forward.

There are several important lessons here. In establishing a direction for the therapy with this couple, I had plenty of information to work with, so I had to choose what I was going to be curious about. For example, when the husband said he didn't know what he wanted to accomplish with the therapy, I could have accepted that answer and moved on. When he said he wasn't able to let go of problems easily, I might have started a new conversation about that issue. If I'd done either of those things, I might never have arrived at an understanding of the direction in which the couple was hoping to go, and I almost certainly wouldn't have gotten to that point in the course of a single session. Instead, we had a conversation directly relevant to the couple's expressed best hopes. At the end of the session, the couple thanked me and asked what the next step would be. I said it was up to them. If they thought a follow-up session would be helpful, I'd be happy to see them. The husband asked his wife if they could return in 2 weeks. She began to cry. She was thrilled he was asking for a follow-up appointment and wondered what had changed his mind. The husband said he'd enjoyed our conversation because it was about looking ahead instead of dwelling on the past. He'd been afraid therapy was going to be focused on things he didn't want to have to deal with again. He was relieved to be moving forward and eager to keep the conversation going.

When the couple returned 2 weeks later, I learned the husband had moved back into the home. He was the first to report how different things had been between the two of them. In that second session, we reviewed the progress and identified each partner's contribution to it. By the end of the hour, the couple believed things had progressed so well, they didn't believe a third session would be needed.

SUMMARY

The solution-focused process seems simple enough. All we're asking is for the clients to explain how they'd like their lives to be different as a result of therapy. It's no more complicated than a taxi driver asking a passenger, "Where to?" Yet, as simple as it seems, the process is not always easy. The therapist will often have to ask multiple questions to move the conversation toward an answer that can work as a direction. Many times, the client will give answers that do not meet the criteria of an effective best hopes answer, and many of those answers will be about the problem.

Therapist: What are your best hopes from this therapy?

Client: We have been fighting for years and years and I think it's because I can't control my temper and she drinks too much.

This is a common kind of answer to the best hopes question, but it's not a useful one. The therapist will have built on the client's response and restate the question. "What would you and your partner be doing other than fighting that would be better for you at the end of this therapy?" This type of question can begin to shift the client's response in a more promising direction.

Often the first answer a couple gives to the best hopes question is filled with problem-saturated language. The therapist must then keep rephrasing the question until a future-focused answer emerges. This step simply must be completed effectively before any subsequent work can be done. It may take a few moments at the beginning of the first session to get an effective best hopes answer, or in rare cases, it may take more than one session. But there's no moving on until it happens.

Step 2:
Connecting With the Couple

"Let us always meet each other with a smile, for the smile is the beginning of love."

—MOTHER TERESA

A few years ago, I met Eve Lipchik, a former core member of the team at the Brief Family Therapy Center in Milwaukee, where the ideas underlying solution-focused therapy originated. Our conversation forever influenced how I would train and write about the solution-focused methodology. She felt that, in the early papers on solution-focused therapy, there was too much emphasis on the techniques involved and not enough emphasis on the relationship between the client and therapist. It's a point Lipchik reiterated in her book, *Beyond Technique in Solution-Focused Therapy: Working with Emotions and the Therapeutic Relationship* (2002).

Before meeting Lipchik, I'd been introduced to the idea of problem-free talk in a training conducted by Chris Iveson at his clinic in London. Many different models of psychotherapy include some form of rapport building by the therapist as part of the process. In solution-focused therapy, rapport building isn't just about establishing a client relationship, it's also about revealing positive aspects of the clients' lives. It allows the therapist to view the individual or the couple as something more than just their problem (George et al., 2006). What follows is a continuation of the dialogue with Michelle and Stephanie. This segment illustrates how the therapist can move from establishing best hopes to problem-free talk.

Therapist: So, before we chat about those things [the best hopes established earlier], is it okay if I get to know the two of you a bit?

Michelle: [Crying] I am very emotional right now because we are really going through a lot, so you will have to forgive me. I'm not just crying here, I cry all day long.

Therapist: You are forgiven. So, is it okay if I spend some time getting to know the two of you before we move on?

Michelle: [No longer crying] Yes.

Stephanie: Yes.

Therapist: Where are you guys from?

Michelle: Louisiana.

Stephanie: Beeville, Texas, a very small town in south Texas.

Therapist: That's a scary part of Texas for me. When I first moved here, I drove down to south Texas to visit a friend, and being from the big city, the dark highways in that part of the state freaked me out a little. Then, out of nowhere, there was this huge glowing statue of Sam Houston that surprised and scared me a little. To this day, when I think about south Texas, I think about that big scary statue.

Michelle: [Laughter]

Stephanie: [Laughter] Yeah, I know exactly where that statue is.

Therapist: Cool. So, how long have you been living in this area?

Stephanie: Ten years. Well, 14 years really, if you count school.

Therapist: What did you go to school for?

Stephanie: To become a teacher. I teach kindergarten.

Therapist: That's a tough job.

Michelle: [Laughter] Yeah, it is! I would kill one of those kids if I had to spend all day with them.

Therapist: [Laughter] Do you like being a kindergarten teacher, Stephanie?

Stephanie: Yeah, I like it a lot. I just don't like the drive to get to my school, which is about 30 miles away. I teach a class with 30 kids, which is large, but because of my work history and experience, the school district assigned me the large class.

Therapist: In a weird way that is somewhat of a compliment. What do you do, Michelle?

Michelle: I actually just switched jobs. I am an office manager for a company that fights insurance companies.

Therapist: You said you just switched jobs. How long ago?

Michelle: About a month.

Therapist: Do you like it?

Michelle: No, I work for my brother and I thought it would be good, but I work like 60 hours a week and I have to travel a lot, which has not been good for us and what we are going through right now.

Therapist: If you could have your dream job, what would that be?

Michelle: You know, I'd like to be in business for myself.

Therapist: Doing what?

Michelle: I'm in school right now working on a degree in business administration.

Therapist: Oh wow!

Michelle: You know? I want to be in the service industry because I love to make people happy. Our thought is to buy a franchise that we know can make us some money to start with, and then, when the economy turns around, open a business that can be ours.

Therapist: Smart ladies, very cool. What else, hmmm. Any kids?

Michelle: Yes, we have a 7-year-old son.

Therapist: What is his name?

Michelle: Edwin.

Therapist: Whose son?

Michelle: Ours. You mean who birthed him?

Therapist: Yes, I apologize for not being more clear.

Michelle: I did.

Therapist: What do you guys do for fun?

Stephanie: Nothing lately.

Therapist: What did you used to do for fun?

Stephanie: We used to like to go to clubs and also play games.

Michelle: [Laughter] Yeah, we used to play video games together a lot.

Stephanie: Yeah, we used to spend hours doing that, we loved it.

Michelle: We even used to go to bars and play the touch screen games they had there.

Stephanie: We also used to go out as a family more often. Like out to eat and stuff like that.

Therapist: It sounds like you guys used to have a lot of fun. So, how long have the two of you been together?

Michelle: Five years.

Stephanie: Yeah, about 5 years.

Therapist: And you live together, is that right?

Michelle: Yes.

Stephanie: Uh-huh.

Therapist: Well, thank you guys for allowing me to get to know some more about you. Do you have questions for me?

Michelle: No.

Stephanie: No.

Therapist: You don't have to have any questions, but I figured I've been pretty nosy about the two of you, so I'll give you the opportunity to be nosy about me if you like.

Michelle: No, I'm okay.

Stephanie: I don't have any questions right now. I did a little research on you online. That pretty much answered all of my questions.

Reading through this dialogue, one might think that the therapist is accomplishing nothing or even wasting valuable session time. In fact, the therapist is working to uncover the positive aspects of the couple's life, and how they were living before their problem. Lipchik (2002) calls this process *listening with a constructive ear*—probing for evidence of strengths, resources, and past success, learning what life was like before or without the problem, what the clients want, or anything at all that can be reinforced as a positive aspect of the client's lives going forward.

When listening with a constructive ear, there are several highlights that stand out in the transcript. The couple clearly has had times when things were working better for them and they were able to discuss those times when asked. They continue to have plans for the future that involve each other, and they're able to work together to accomplish goals (planning to open a business together, raising a child, and having one partner working on a degree). Still, beyond these and other positive insights that came to light in our rapport-building conversation, the couple's demeanor was transformed during this part of the discussion. They went from being very emotional, with one partner crying and saying more than once that, "We're going through a lot right now," to smiling and no longer interested in discussing problems. By listening with a constructive ear, I could see that the more interested I became in the two of them as people, the more personable each of them became. It was an interesting dynamic that is not at all uncommon in this phase of therapy.

THE THERAPIST'S TASK IN DEVELOPING A CONNECTION

When I first observed a practitioner conducting solution-focused therapy, it seemed beyond simple. The therapist was working with a family on a very complicated problem, but it was somehow transformed into an issue with a very obvious solution. In making it happen, the therapist did little more than ask simple questions. It seemed remarkably easy, but when it came time for me to replicate the process, I realized it was no such thing. The therapist was working hard to elicit information that could later assist in the solution-building process. The therapist was listening for the following.

Past Successes

Every couple comes from a past when the relationship was working much better. They come into therapy as a team with at least some common history. They must have done some work to build themselves into a successful couple at the beginning of their relationship. The therapist listens for clues about how the relationship was built to understand what worked in the past and continues to work today. This can be difficult because the partners may be so immersed in their current problem that they're genuinely unable to recall any past successes. But the information is there, and the therapist's task is to ask the questions that uncover it.

Systemic Resources

People facing problems in their lives tend to be more aware of their flaws and shortcomings than their talents. A couple living through difficulties may be too unhappy and distracted to notice possible pathways toward solutions. The therapist's role is to listen for evidence of the strengths, talents, and successes of an individual or a couple who can be brought to realize their best hopes. The positive resources are there, and they can lead toward solutions. The clients need only to be made aware of them.

Descriptions of the Relationship
Before or Without the Problem

I've often heard the phrase, *the devil is in the details*, but in working with couples, *the beauty is in the details* seems more apt. The more details that can be uncovered about what a couple's life was like before the problem, the more those details can contribute to the solution-building process. Eliciting this kind of information is difficult because it's not the information that has led the couple into therapy, and it's not likely to be top-of-mind for them. The task is to bring this information forward and make it as memorable as the current problem. When couples come to therapy, they're often prepared to discuss problems and are able to give a detailed description of the problems to the therapist. But the information that's of interest to a solution-focused therapist is something else entirely.

What the Client Really Wants

The most important thing for the therapist to be listening for isn't just what the client wants, but what they *really* want. When couples come to my office and we discuss their best hopes for therapy, I often get what I call a minimum answer—an answer based on their smallest hopes rather than their biggest dreams. For example, a couple may say, "We just don't want to be fighting anymore." Such an answer may suffice in some forms of therapy, but the solution-focused practitioner is looking for more specific information. "What would you most want to replace the fighting when you are able to successfully remove that from your relationship?" This question shifts the couple's language from the absence of the problem to the presence of the solution. That's the answer the therapist should be listening to hear.

JOHN AND STACY

John and Stacy are a couple I remember fondly. John was a nice but very quiet man on first meeting, while Stacy was a live wire. In working with them to establish best hopes for therapy, Stacy had a great deal to say and John had very little to add. In the process of getting to know them better, Stacy continued to carry the conversation and John remained mostly quiet. When I asked the couple if they had questions for me, I noticed that John loosened up and became more engaged. At the end of the session, I asked John and Stacy what they'd found helpful in our conversation. John said he'd really appreciated that I took the time to get to know them and that I'd offered to answer their questions. He said that he and Stacy had visited a therapist in the past and it had been a very different experience. John's answer surprised me because, although I'd offered to answer any questions he might have, he hadn't asked any. It seemed that just having the opportunity to ask was enough for him to feel connected and respected.

I'm not sure why I got in the habit of offering clients the opportunity to question me, but because my job was to ask so many questions of them, it seemed only fair. I was surprised that this was what John had found most helpful in our sessions and had provided the foundation for our later work, but it serves as a reminder of how motivation increases when a couple feels connected to the therapist. In the following weeks, I met with John and Stacy three more times, and the couple progressed to the point where they felt their best hopes had been realized. As I look back on what they accomplished in such a short time, I'm thankful I'd made that all-important connection with John.

SUMMARY

One of the most trying aspects of training professionals to work with couples using solution-focused therapy is expecting professionals to go slowly and to develop a connection with their couples before moving on. To me, this is the art of working as a therapist, and it lays the groundwork for effective interventions later on. It takes discipline because, at this point in the process, clients are apt to say intriguing things that may lead the therapist astray. Couples often bring high levels of anxiety and pain into treatment, and all come with a history. The history can be addressed as the conversation unfolds, but if the therapist is too eager to delve into this information at the outset, the conversation can easily become saturated with problems, making a solution-building conversation much more difficult.

I've come to believe that individuals and couples come to therapy prepared to explain their problems not because they believe that's what will be most helpful to them, but because they think it's information the therapist needs. Most people believe that solutions are directly connected to problems, so the notion that therapy can be successful without a discussion of the problem seems counterintuitive. However, the fact is, I've never had clients who wanted to return to the problem once we'd begun a conversation about their successes, resources, and hopes for the future.

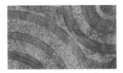

Step 3:
Honeymoon Talk

Reviewing a Couple's Successful Past

"Memories are the key not to the past, but to the future."
—Corrie ten Boom

In the parlance of therapists, exceptions are those times when clients unconsciously do something positive in their lives in spite of their problem, opening up pathways toward potential solutions. The idea of exceptions has been a part of solution-focused therapy (SFT) from the very beginning. The SFT team in Milwaukee worked to understand how people break problem patterns and move toward solutions (de Shazer, 1985), and this principle is applicable to couples as well as individuals. There are always times when troubled couples behave as if there were no problem, doing things that are incongruent with their problem story. Because we know that at one time they chose to come together and build a relationship, we know that their past must be riddled with exceptions that are worth exploring by the therapist.

Here is more of my conversation with Michelle and Stephanie:

Therapist: So, you told me you have been together for 5 years, but how did you meet?

Michelle: [Laughing] At a club.

Stephanie: [Laughing] A club that we normally don't even go to.

Michelle: It sounds like we do a lot of clubbing but we really don't, it was more like a little pub than a club.

Therapist: So, you met at a little pub?

Michelle: [Laughing] No, we met at a club. It was actually a straight club and some friends asked me to come out with them, so I agreed.

Stephanie: And I had just gotten out of a relationship, so I was just out and about by myself.

Therapist: Who noticed who first?

Michelle: I noticed her.

Therapist: I know we are going back 5 years here, but what was it about Stephanie that you noticed?

Michelle: Her swag. The way she walked around. It was just so sexy.

Therapist: Wow, you answered that in like a nanosecond! It was her swag that you noticed?

Michelle: Yes, it was just her *everything*, the way she looked around.

Therapist: What was so sexy about it?

Michelle: Everything. The way she dressed, the way she looked, her facial expressions.

Therapist: Stephanie, when did you notice Michelle?

Michelle: I stopped traffic that night.

Stephanie: Yeah, everyone in the club noticed her that night. I was sitting at a table with some people I didn't know, because remember I was there by myself, kind of close to the door, and she walks in and stopped everyone and said, "What's your name?"

Therapist: Wait a minute, you did that?

Michelle: [Laughing] Uh huh.

Stephanie: And I was just shocked, like who is this person who would stop everything just to try and talk to me? It kind of intrigued me. It made me want to find out more about her.

Therapist: As you found out more about her that night, what did you like about her?

Michelle: [Laughing] I was sexy.

Stephanie: Yeah, but it was more than that, she was attractive and it really surprised me.

Michelle: She remembers what I had on that night.

Stephanie: Yeah, to this day I know exactly what she had on.

Therapist: Do you really? How did you show her that you were attracted to her?

Stephanie: Um, she was dancing a bit later and I just started dancing with her. Well, there was a big incident.

Michelle: [Laughing]

Stephanie: My ex somehow showed up at the club and got between us, and after the incident, I went back to Michelle and apologized.

Michelle: I thought it was her girlfriend and I was like, "Oops, my bad." But she apologized and promised it was her ex.

Therapist: You went back to apologize?

Stephanie: Yeah, I just wanted to let her know that it was my ex and to give her my phone number. I just wanted to make sure that someone from my past didn't ruin anything. I don't know why my ex did that, but I didn't want her to scare off someone I wanted to get to know.

Therapist: Yeah, so how long did it take for the two of you to create a relationship?

Michelle: March 24; it took us about a month or so.

Therapist: What was working so well in the beginning?

Michelle: We did everything together.

Therapist: What type of stuff did you do?

Michelle: Everything, we would go to the grocery store, go to the mall, take my son places; I mean everything we did, we did together. It wasn't separate like our lives are right now.

Stephanie: Yeah, she lived in Haslet and I lived in Dallas. That is a long way and I would travel every day, or at least every weekend, to see her. I would rush home from work just so I could hurry and go see her.

Therapist: That's a lot of driving.

Stephanie: [Laughing] I know.

Therapist: Were the two of you happy then?

Michelle: Yes.

Stephanie: Yes.

Therapist: If I had been friends with the two of you then, how would I have known you were happy?

Michelle: Because we were smiling all the time, we just had that glow that comes along with having that in-love feeling.

Therapist: Stephanie, same question; if we were friends back then, how would I have known you were happy?

Stephanie: You would have never seen me.

Michelle: [Laughing]

Stephanie: [Laughing] You would have been mad and jealous because I was never around, I was always with her.

Therapist: [Laughing] So, I would not have seen you much. If I caught you on the phone, how would you have described your relationship?

[At this point in the session, Michelle placed her hand on Stephanie's leg and it remained there for much of the rest of the session.]

Stephanie: It was going good, real good.

Therapist: How long did that last?

Michelle: It didn't really get bad until recently. She may have a different thought about that though.

Stephanie: I would have to say 4 years.

Therapist: Wow, you guys were able to keep the happiness going for 4 years?

Stephanie: Yeah, it just got really bad about a year ago.

Therapist: How did you guys keep the happiness going for so long?

Michelle: I don't know. For me, it is that she is so good to me. I am truly spoiled rotten. You know, I just know that she truly loves me, there are no conditions on it. Even when I gained a lot of weight, it didn't change anything.

Therapist: So her ability to unconditionally love you helped keep things going so well for so long?

Michelle: Yeah, absolutely.

Therapist: Stephanie, what would you say it was about Michelle that kept it going for so long?

Michelle: I can't wait to hear this answer.

Stephanie: It was her personality and I always know she has my back. Her actions have just shown me that she genuinely cares for my well-being. She loves me and she is there for me. And of course her son; I just love being a family.

Notice that the therapist is quite interested in the details of the relationship when it was working better for each partner. Every detail is important because there's no way of knowing which detail will be the one that unlocks the couple's pathway to a different future experience. When Michelle put her hand on Stephanie's leg and left it there, it was in direct contrast to the beginning of the session, when Michelle seemed determined to speak about the problem. Once the details of the couple's successful past came out, she became more emotional and more connected, and her actions followed her words. The positive feelings were so strong that the very notion of discussing the problem at that point seemed foreign and destructive to all parties in the room.

THE THERAPIST'S TASKS IN
EXPLORING THE SUCCESSFUL PAST

The task of the therapist when reviewing a couple's successful past is to identify and discuss even the most intimate details of that time in their lives. The beauty lies in the details and it's the therapist's role to be curious about them. Many couples who come to therapy have experienced a significant or traumatic problem that has affected both members in some way or another. In most cases, the problem has caused the couple to forget that their relationship had been working well at some earlier time or caused them to lose hope that they will ever be able to get back to the happy lives they once enjoyed. By having a conversation with them about the good times in their past, the positive aspects of those days are invited into the present where they can have a positive effect.

Years ago, the facilitator at a conference on SFT told me that one of the things he liked about the approach is that the clients are highly motivated. He wasn't saying that clients receiving SFT are somehow more motivated than the clients receiving other kinds of therapy. His point was that, in the process of answering solution-focused questions, clients tap into the best of themselves and their experiences, which increases their motivation. In working with couples, a therapist must always remember that the couple has at least some level of motivation that prompted them into attending the session. I've had several couples tell me that the only reason they came into therapy was, "So, we [or I] can say we tried everything" prior to divorce—as if divorce was a foregone conclusion and therapy was merely a step along the way. Although that may be true in some cases, it's also true that the couple would not be in therapy if there were not some degree of hope left in them. Hope is what the therapist must bring into the conversation.

The therapist's goal should not be just to identify the details of the couple's successful past, but to invite the clients to take credit for that success. That may seem to be easy enough, despite the fact that most people are more reluctant to take credit for their successes than they are to take blame for their failures. It's almost as if they believe that the past was positive because of some external factors that cannot be changed or returned to. A couple might explain that they were happy in the past because they had time to concentrate on each other and build their relationship, but with the arrival of kids or increasing responsibilities at work, that was no longer possible. That may be true and accurate, but it gives all the credit for a successful past to circumstances and not to what the couple had managed to accomplish within those circumstances.

HOW DID YOU MEET?

One of the most helpful questions I ask couples in exploring their past successes is, "How did you meet?" Answering this simple question invites the couple into a conversation about the positive past instead of the current problem. I began routinely asking this question after I noticed a trend in the way couples tend to answer it. One of the first couples I asked had been married for several years but were considering divorce because of infidelity and other problems. It was clear that there was a tremendous amount of hurt and resentment between them. In our first session, the partners took turns blaming each other for the problems in their relationship. There was yelling, name calling, and at one point, the wife threatened to walk out of the session. Despite my best efforts, I could not end the arguing or stop the hurtful comments. My instinct was to end the session myself, because it was going nowhere and was potentially doing more harm than good. But before I did, I remembered to ask the question that had once worked so well for me, "How did you two meet?"

The couple's demeanor changed almost instantly. They smiled as they recounted the story of how they got together. Everything about them changed—their body language, their tone of voice, the content of the conversation—as they told me one of the most beautiful and romantic stories I've ever heard. As the details of their meeting emerged, it was almost as if they'd somehow been transported back in time. Each partner took some credit for building their relationship in the beginning. When they returned for a second session, they reported significant progress and credited the retelling of the details of their early days as the catalyst.

It's now become a standard practice for me to ask the couples how they met and, almost without exception, the results are similar. Every couple makes the choice to be together at some point, and it stands to reason that the choice was based on some sort of mutually recognized compatibility. That's what I aim to help the couples rediscover.

TAKING CREDIT FOR SUCCESS

People often tell me that the trouble they're experiencing in their relationship is due to some personal trait they possess or lack, while attributing any successes to external factors. We were happy before we had kids, or before we moved, or before we changed jobs. Yet, when invited to take credit for the good as well as the bad times in their lives, people will that invitation and build on it.

Patrick and Allison came to see me because they'd been drifting apart in recent years. Patrick was a poor communicator (according to Allison), and Allison was a nag (according to Patrick), but both reported that they'd been close and happy until Patrick started his own business several years ago. The business had grown into quite a success, employing dozens of people, and accounting for all of the couple's income. In the first session, Patrick explained that he devotes 100% of his energy to the business, and that he is often not in the best of moods when he comes home from work. Allison said that because she's home all day caring for their young child, she craves adult conversation, and when Patrick isn't willing to talk to her, she gets frustrated and nags him. The couple was eloquent in their understanding of the problems between them, but when I asked them to describe what their relationship was like from their first meeting to their happiest moment, they seemed much less knowledgeable. Yet, as the details of their past successes came out, Patrick and Allison were able to take credit for their successes by answering questions such as, "How did you do that?" or "How did you let your partner know you were pleased?" In answering those questions out loud, they were taking and giving credit for their successes and identifying the strengths of each other and their relationship. The assignment the couple agreed to take on between sessions was to develop a list of traits and characteristics that each possessed that led to the relationship's early success, and to notice how those traits and characteristics played a role in their lives during the week.

On the day of the second session, Patrick and Allison had a different look about them—they seemed to be happier and more loving toward each other. They reported that they'd had their best week in years. Both partners felt they were being respected and heard, and there had been a significant decrease in the behaviors that led them into counseling. When asked how they had made such changes in only a week, they attributed it to the work that was done in the first session—how helpful it had been to recall how they'd built their relationship before Patrick started his business and what each of their roles had been in the process. According to Patrick, they hadn't told anyone the story of their early days in years and had never thought about what their roles had been in creating the happiness of the past. Now that they were aware of what they'd done in the past that worked, doing those things in the present became easier.

SAY IT OUT LOUD

Recently, I was addressing a couple's group and someone asked me why so many marriages fail. Although I think that question is far too sweeping for me to answer, I do have a few thoughts. One is that, when we spend enough time with another person, we begin to feel as if we know them and they know us, which leads us to make assumptions. In reviewing the successful past and allowing ourselves to say things out loud, we sometimes discover those assumptions to be inaccurate—we may even discover that our false assumptions have led us to discontinue positive, helpful behaviors. In the case of Patrick and Allison, they'd come into the first session prepared to discuss the problems that led them into therapy, and it was clear that they were quite knowledgeable about those issues. However, when asked what they'd done to win their partner's heart, the answers were more difficult to come by. In fact, each admitted that they'd never before asked that question of each other. It's not an uncommon response, but it surprises me every time I hear it. For years, this couple had been discussing the nature of their problem and what each partner's perceived role in the problem had been. Since they didn't agree on the nature of the problem or their partner's perception of their role in it, their discussions devolved into arguments that were destructive to the relationship. Neither of them had ever asked what behaviors had attracted them to each other in the first place. When that question was posed to them in my office, the partners were able to learn for the first time what made them work well together as a couple. By saying these things out loud, each partner was hearing compliments about their past conduct and learning new information about what their partner likes.

Some couples therapists—particularly the ones who practice from a problem-focused perspective—believe that one shortcoming of solution-focused therapy is that it ignores the past. That's not entirely accurate. Although it's true that the solution-focused approach looks toward the future and requires that the practitioner have an understanding of the use of future-focused questions, that's largely because couples often misunderstand their own histories. As de Shazer (see Zeig & Gilligan, 1990) has pointed out, although a couple's past may contain many successes, those positives tend to be overlooked as a couple struggles to understand what's currently going wrong. When a solution-focused therapist asks a couple to look backward, it must be to the successful past and not the more troubled immediate one.

THE SOLUTION-FOCUSED CLOSET

A few years ago, my sessions with a couple in their mid- to late forties illustrated the process of successfully exploring the past in solution-focused conversations quite clearly. After the couple's third session, they felt that their hopes had been realized and decided that they needed no further appointments. About a month later, I got a phone call from the husband asking me to describe the type of therapy he'd just been through. He said he couldn't believe the changes he and his wife had been able to make, and that the changes had persisted. We chatted for a while and he said he was going to send me something in the mail. A week later, I received a letter from him titled, "The Solution-Focused Closet." Because there are details in the letter that would violate the couple's confidentiality, I cannot print the letter here, but I can share the general theme. The husband wrote that the aspect of the sessions he and his wife most enjoyed was the time spent reviewing their past—how they'd fallen in love and what each of their roles in that process had been. He said that it had been a long time since they'd recalled the feelings they'd once had for one another and how helpful it had been to review them and take credit for them. He compared this experience to that of opening a closet in preparation for a trip. He noted that everyone has things in their closet that they have no plans to throw out, yet for one reason or another they'll never wear again. These items get very little attention, even though we see them every day as we hunt for our favorite clothes to wear. When packing for a vacation, we don't take the whole closet; we sort through the clothes for the ones that will make us look our best, leaving the others behind. The husband said that in the course of our solution-focused conversations, he and his wife realized that they didn't have to take all of their bad memories with them into the future—but they didn't have to discard them either. Instead they can simply leave them hanging undisturbed in the closet of their past. In our sessions, this couple learned to select the parts of the past they wanted to experience going forward, creating a hopeful, promising future for their marriage. He ended his letter by thanking me, but I was even more thankful to both of them.

BACK FROM THE BRINK

Aaron and Melinda are a dynamic couple that I worked with recently; helping them to mend their relationship and get back on track and to be happy with one another again. When I first met them, they were sitting on opposite couches in my lobby, as many new-client couples tend to do. It's common for couples to come for the first session in a less enthusiastic mood, and Aaron and Melinda were an extreme example. Melinda made it clear at the outset that she was very upset with Aaron and no longer respected him as a man or a husband. With profane language and frequent insults, Melinda said that Aaron was not the man he used to be. He was now fat, depressed, and had put her through the toughest times of her life.

Aaron's demeanor was quiet as the session began. He seemed sad. He said he just wanted to get things back to when he and his wife were happy.

In getting to know them, I learned that Melinda had grown up in financially difficult circumstances. One of her greatest fears as an adult was going broke and, unfortunately, that's just what happened. Aaron had been a successful business owner, but when the economy went sour, his company quickly went under. The family lost everything—their home, cars, and everything. Despite that, and the obvious anger she was feeling, Melinda still seemed to love and respect her husband on a basic level. It was clear that Aaron still loved and respected Melinda, and missed the way things used to be between the two of them. It was the details of how this couple functioned in the good times that led to the solution that eventually saved their marriage.

Every time I see a couple change their marriage for the better, I'm amazed. Many times, it takes only a simple solution to resolve serious, long-standing problems. The solutions developed in the therapeutic process are often a surprise to the couples themselves, and that was the case with Aaron and Melinda.

The more I asked about the details of the past when things were happier between them, the more they began to exhibit happiness right there in my office. The tone of the conversation changed, especially in the way Melinda talked to Aaron. Her voice grew softer and, eventually, she actually paid him a compliment. She said that even though he had experienced significant professional hardships, he was rebuilding the family's finances. The moment Melinda said that, Aaron began to cry. "I didn't think she noticed how hard I was working."

Melinda continued to compliment Aaron, letting him know that not only had she noticed how hard he was working, but that she appreciated how difficult a job it was for him and how good he was becoming at it. In the years following the collapse of his business, Aaron worked as a salesman for a medical supply company, and despite his lack of experience and a natural affinity for sales, he'd been doing quite well. When asked how he'd managed to do it, Aaron explained that when he arrived for a sales call, he'd sit in his car beforehand and remind himself that no matter how hard he found sales to be, it was not as tough as letting his family down.

As the session continued, we were able to move on to more future-focused language. The stage had been properly set by a thorough examination of the couple's successful past. The first time I saw Aaron and Melinda, there had been so much anger and so many hurt feelings, and there could be no conversation about a preferred future at that moment. In the course of the session, it became clear that Aaron and Melinda were thinking and talking about things in ways that were new to them. It didn't take long for them to realize that this new way of thinking and talking was working better for them, and we soon moved on to a discussion about what the future would be like if the successful past could re-create itself. By the end of the session, the couple's demeanor was visibly different.

When Aaron and Melinda arrived for their second session two weeks later, it was obvious that the changes realized in the first session had endured. The couple was all smiles and laughter in the lobby, and once in my office, they reported significant progress. There had been no arguing between sessions, and the couple had been intimate for the first time in months. Aaron and Melinda thought things were going so well, they saw no point in scheduling further sessions. A few months later, I got a letter from them with an enclosed photograph of a house. They wrote that they had managed to rebuild their relationship and finances—and had bought their dream home. There have been a few moments in my work that have brought me to tears, and this was one of them.

FINDING EXCEPTIONS

Exceptions are those times when clients do something unrelated to their problem. Steve de Shazer (1985) described this as "not following the problem rule." Instead, clients behave, often unconsciously, as if their problem does not exist. For example, a couple may make a statement like, "We need to learn how to communicate." They may use the language of absolutes in expressing their desire for better communication, as in, "We don't know how to agree," or, "We've never gotten along." Of course, it's almost always true that the couple does in fact know how to communicate, agree, and get along—they've just never given themselves credit for it. If they truly did not know how to communicate, how could they manage to successfully divide the parenting tasks in the household, or even decide what they'll have for dinner every night? How could they decide to pursue therapy or agree on a therapist? Exceptions provide the kind of information in which a solution-focused practitioner should be interested, because when clients forget to follow the problem rule, they open potential pathways to solutions that can resolve the current problems.

Because exceptions frequently occur without the person being aware of them, it's the therapist's task to assist in identifying and amplifying those moments, thereby helping the couple learn from those behaviors to develop their own solutions. The good news is that there are always exceptions in working with couples. Few people would dispute the fact that there are no perfect couples, but if that's true, then the opposite must also be true: there are no perfectly imperfect couples either. Every great couple must have some sort of flaw, and every flawed couple must have some sort of greatness. For that reason, spending time in identifying and amplifying these exceptions is a crucial step in applying the solution-focused approach to couples therapy. Spending time in attending to these exceptions and to the couple's successful times before identifying a preferred future changes the direction of the conversation. Taking time early in the conversation to review the positive aspects of the couple's lives has an almost instant effect on the couple and on the way they communicate in the session. Upset partners become collaborative. Individuals skeptical of therapy become hopeful. People much prefer a conversation about their strengths and resources than to a discussion of their flaws. Shifting the emphasis allows the conversation to move on to the next step—the preferred future—creating an environment for a more meaningful conversation to follow.

SUMMARY

People are brilliant, and we create our relationships brilliantly. Yet somehow, when trouble arises in a relationship, we forget our brilliance— the very thing that's needed to resolve the problem and move forward. The role of honeymoon talk in solution-focused therapy is to re-establish brilliance by reviewing past successes and allowing each partner to take credit for those successes. The task sounds simple enough, but as we've seen, simple does not always mean easy. Taking credit for one's brilliance is often a new way of thinking, and it's almost always the exact opposite of the conversation the couple was expecting to have when they decided to seek therapy.

Solution-focused therapy has long been described as an approach to counseling that focuses on the future, but I find that description is incomplete. Examining a couple's past is an incredibly powerful step in the therapeutic process that allows an eventual conversation about the future to happen in a more helpful and effective way. Discussing a successful past often drastically changes the mood of the conversation. It is almost as if couples transform themselves back into people who were previously happy and in love. This change allows the therapist to have a conversation about the future from the standpoint of happiness, rather than a starting point of despair.

Step 4:
The Preferred Future

Envisioning the Best Tomorrow

*"My interest is in the future because I am going to spend the rest of my
life there."*

—CHARLES F. KETTERING

One of the greatest contributions by the team at the Brief Family Therapy
Center in Milwaukee is their emphasis on the future, and perhaps the
most famous element of their many innovative techniques is the *miracle
question*. It was originally posed by Steve de Shazer:

> Suppose that one night while you were asleep, there was a mira-
> cle and this problem was solved. How would you know? What
> would be different? How would your husband know without you
> saying a word to him about it? (de Shazer, 1988)

The miracle question is a type of future-focused question a therapist
can use to help shift the focus and language of a couple's conversation
from the current problem to a conversation on a future without the problem. Shifting the conversation in this way seems to be a simple matter, but
accomplishing it requires discipline. To demonstrate the process of asking

the miracle question to a couple in session, I'll continue my dialogue with Michelle and Stephanie.

Therapist: Suppose by some chance you woke up tomorrow and that in-love feeling you have been describing to me, that glow, was back. How would you notice it? If it just happened overnight somehow, what would be your very first clue?

Michelle: I wouldn't wake up crying.

Therapist: What would you be doing instead?

Michelle: I would be smiling and happy, all hugs and kisses.

Therapist: Which of you tends to wake up first?

Stephanie: I do.

Michelle: Because I work from home most days.

Therapist: So, Stephanie, since you are the first one to wake, what would first give you the idea that something was different?

Stephanie: About her or about me?

Therapist: Either.

Stephanie: Well, probably she would wake up and say good-bye or I love you [when I left for work] or something like that.

Therapist: What would be different about the way she says good-bye or I love you on this day compared to other days when she has said similar things?

Stephanie: It would be an extra minute longer, a deeper kiss.

Therapist: How would you respond to that?

Stephanie: I would return it with the same type of kiss. This is the type of thing that would make me want to do something for her, like bring her flowers or something like that.

Therapist: So, if on this day for some reason you decide to give Stephanie an extra-minute hug and kiss and she responds with an extra kiss, would that be odd to you?

Michelle: Yes, it would be so wonderful. Just the intimacy would be amazing, nothing sexual, but just that closeness.

Therapist: So, if this actually happened, how would Stephanie let you know she had noticed?

Michelle: She would smile. When she is happy she smiles a lot and giggles.

Therapist: So she would be giggling at you?

Michelle: Yeah, she would be giggling a lot.

Therapist: What would this giggle mean to you?

Michelle: That she is happy and that she feels good. The look in her eyes would be different.

Therapist: What would be different about the look in her eyes?

Michelle: She would not be sad.

Therapist: What would she be instead of sad?

Michelle: Happy. She has a different look in her eyes when she is happy.

Therapist: Is that something you would notice?

Michelle: Absolutely.

Therapist: How would you let her know that you noticed it?

Michelle: I would just hug her a little tighter.

Therapist: In what way would these events be different from the way things have been recently?

Michelle: This is so different. When I am not happy and we are not happy, there's nothing. There is none of this. Things are very cold between us. Almost like we are barking orders at each other like, "Get up," and things like that.

Therapist: Good, so this would be different. So Stephanie, what would be a sign to you as you began your trip to work that these differences were following you?

Stephanie: She would call me and say I hope you have a great day, or maybe we can do something later. You know, an invitation to spend time together.

Therapist: How would you let her know that you were pleased to receive this call?

Stephanie: I would just come out and say it. I don't know what else I would do.

Therapist: Michelle, would that be nice to hear from her?

Michelle: Oh yes, I would let her know that I wanted us to cook dinner together when we both got home from work. I used to cook but I don't cook very much anymore.

Therapist: So Michelle, how would you know that, as you began your work day, these good things were continuing?

Michelle: Because I would be thinking about her more in a happy way, like I used to before we started having all of these problems. I would also be texting her nice things throughout the day too and, like she said, we would be talking on the way to work.

Therapist: You said something about happy thoughts. What happy thoughts would be going through your head?

Michelle: That I love her and I miss her. How nice it was to feel good again.

Therapist: How would you share these happy thoughts with Stephanie?

Michelle: I am just a very intimate person when I am happy, so it would just roll off in everything that I do and everything that I say. My happiness affects everything that I do—my job, my kid, and my everything.

Therapist: Who would be the first to notice that you had become happy?

Michelle: Everyone in my house.

Therapist: What would be their first clue that you had become happy all of a sudden?

Michelle: That I am not screaming at everyone and the dog, just that I am not hateful.

Therapist: What would you be instead?

Michelle: Smiling, laughing, and loving.

Therapist: Would that be more like the real you?

Michelle: Yeah.

Therapist: [To Stephanie] What would the kids in your classroom notice about you that would tell them you are having a different kind of day? One of my favorite things about kids is how perceptive they can be.

Stephanie: That is so true. When I am happy I am so much more patient with them, and they always ask what is going on at those times.

Therapist: So, this would stand out to them in some way?

Stephanie: Yes, I would be smiling at them and more playful and more patient with them when they act up. It would be so much better.

Therapist: And would that be more like the real you?

Stephanie: Yes, that would.

Therapist: And when you got off work and reached home, what would be the first sign that this miracle was continuing?

Stephanie: By her facial expression, closeness, and body language. That's how I would know.

Therapist: Interesting. What would her facial expression be?

Stephanie: Hmm, smiling.

Therapist: So just smiling would be the clue?

Stephanie: Yeah, and she would give me a hug.

Therapist: What would stand out about this hug that would let you know things were going well?

Stephanie: It would be a both-hand hug, a rub-the-back hug, or a tight hug.

Therapist: [To Michelle] Is that a Michelle-at-her-best hug?

Stephanie: Yeah.

Michelle: Yes.

Therapist: What would you be noticing about Stephanie on this day that would be making you smile and hug her like that?

Michelle: Her smile and her expression. She would be smiling, and this little grin that she has would be back.

Therapist: Would you notice that little grin if it were to return?

Michelle: Oh yes.

Therapist: And you mentioned a hug as well. Tell me about the hug you would receive on this day.

Michelle: She would put both arms around me and squeeze so tight, almost like she's trying to pick me up.

Therapist: You once mentioned that you might be going out to eat on this day, where might you go?

Michelle: I'd say Pappadeuxs, I love seafood.

Stephanie: Then that is where we would go. When we are at our best, she tends to get her way more often and I just accommodate.

Michelle: That is true.

Therapist: What would be different about this dinner that would let the two of you know that you were still back on track?

Michelle: We would be sitting next to each other and not across from each other. The conversation would be different; we would be talking again.

Therapist: What would you be talking about?

Michelle: Who knows, who cares? We would be talking about everything and anything.

Stephanie: Future plans. Things about our son, like should we put him in basketball, or about our future business.

Therapist: This would be different?

Michelle: Yes it would, right now conversations are not about the future and very tense.

Therapist: Also, you mentioned earlier that when you first met you noticed her swagger and were quite attracted to her. Would that be part of the conversation as well?

Michelle: Yes, and I would tell her that I was attracted to her once again. I have this look that I do and she would definitely notice that.

Stephanie: Yes, I would definitely see it.

Michelle: Sex would also be a very big sign, since recently there hasn't been very much of that.

Therapist: If I get too personal I apologize and feel free not to answer any question that I ask, but how would you know that this would be a day when sex would happen?

Michelle: Me going to bed with a sexy nightie on.

Stephanie: Yeah, I would notice that.

Therapist: Would that be the type of thing that you would do to wrap up a day like this?

Michelle: It would be wonderful to end the day close and holding each other.

Watching the tape of this session, I was moved by something that the words alone don't capture. As the details of the preferred future were being discussed, the couple began to smile and look at each other. There was frequent laughter and touching between them. The presence of hope was very much growing throughout the conversation, and all of us in the room could feel it. Later in the session, it became even more clear.

IT'S SIMPLE

I've said that one of the things that most appeals to me about solution-focused (SF) therapy is its simplicity, and one of the things I've come to realize is it's simple enough that we all have the skills to practice it. I mentioned earlier in the text that this approach is so simple that it is complicated. This is because this approach does not require the therapist to investigate the origins of a problem. In order to stick to a description of the "future" a therapist must have the discipline to refrain from following the client's lead toward the use of "problem language." This is the root of the complexity, because most clinicians were trained to pursue this kind of background information. From an early age, we all come to understand that a conversation is built by people taking turns, each contributing equally to the dialogue, and that's all there is to building solutions within couples. Of course, it takes discipline for the therapist to resist the urge to interrupt when one member of the couple says something interesting, and it requires focus and attention to detail to ensure that each person is allowed to contribute equally. Look again at this short excerpt from the conversation with Michelle and Stephanie:

Stephanie: By her facial expression, closeness, and body language. That's how I would know.

Therapist: Interesting. What would her facial expression be?

Stephanie: Hmm, smiling.

Therapist: So, just smiling would be the clue?

Notice that each of the therapist's responses uses data from what the client has said. This ensures that the conversation does not go in a direction in which the client would not approve. Also, notice how many times the therapist asks questions like, "Would that be pleasing to you?" or "Would that be different?" This is another way to ensure that the questions being asked are meaningful to the client. It's also a way to amplify differences between the preferred future description and whatever is currently going on in the couple's relationship. If the client responds positively to such questions, then the difference has been noticed, and we can continue building the preferred future description. If a client responds by saying no—that particular detail would not be pleasing or different—it's a clue to the therapist that the conversation is not moving in a direction that would make a difference to the client, and a new direction is needed.

THE THERAPIST'S TASK IN
DETERMINING THE PREFERRED FUTURE

I can sum up the therapist's task during this phase in the conversation with one word: curiosity. To uncover a detailed description of a preferred future, the therapist's role is to remain a curious observer, thereby helping the couple uncover even the smallest details. This is the most important part of the conversation—everything said up to this point has been intended to enable a detailed description of a future without the problem and everything that comes later will build on this work. The job now is to amass as many details as possible—you can never have too many!

The process of gathering details about a preferred future is therapeutic in itself. Often nothing more needs to happen for the couple to make significant and lasting changes in their lives and in their relationship, and the more thorough their description of their future, the more good it's likely to do.

Most couples come to therapy seeking the absence of a problem. Suppose a couple says they'd like to be "fighting less." If the therapist allows that to become the direction, the session will be about the problem and little will be accomplished. Imagine instead that the therapist helps the couple replace "fighting less" with something else entirely, say "trust" or "intimacy." That will be a very different conversation—one that describes a future world the couple can begin to experience almost immediately.

A WELL-DEVELOPED PREFERRED
FUTURE . . .

. . . Must Be *About* the Future

To underscore the obvious, a workable description of the preferred future must in fact be about the future, even though a couple may do their very best to draw the therapist into a rehashing of the past. When asked about their hopes for therapy, partners may seek resolution for some past event, as in,

"I need to get over being hurt by my spouse last summer." In other forms of therapy, that may be an appropriate aim for a therapeutic intervention. In solution-focused therapy, the aim must be restated as a future description. That can be as simple as inviting the partners to tell you about their future. By asking questions that begin with *suppose* and contain *will*, the therapist can launch a conversation about a future without the problem. "Suppose you were over this hurt from last summer, how will you notice it?" The response will be about noticing signs in the future, not about the past.

In working with Michelle and Stephanie, the change in their demeanor when we began discussing a future without the problem was noticeable. They spoke in much softer tones, they sat closer together, and began to enjoy saying things that made the other partner happy. It was almost as if they'd already begun living in a future world where both partners are happy.

Keeping the conversation centered on solutions instead of the problem doesn't mean ignoring the problem. On the contrary, every problem needs to be acknowledged—doing anything else would be disrespectful to the client. But the conversation must be carefully crafted so that the solution, rather than the problem, gets the attention. When a problem comes up, it must be acknowledged and accepted by the therapist. But the next question must be about what the future would look like without it.

. . . Must Be Mathematically Positive

I'll let you in on a little secret; I'm terrible at math. My skills don't reliably extend far beyond simply knowing the difference between plus and minus. A plus sign is positive and indicates the presence of something, of course, whereas a minus sign is negative and indicates the absence of something. Although couples may come to therapy hoping for the *absence* of a problem, the job of a solution-focused therapist is to steer them in a more positive direction—toward a future with the *presence* of a solution. When people say that SFT is a *positive* methodology, they usually mean it in the hopeful, rosy, optimistic sense of the word. But it's also positive in the mathematical sense—it's about the presence of a solution and not the absence of a problem.

Insoo Kim Berg has said that one of the most important words in solution-focused therapy is *instead*. By using the word instead, the therapist can shift a client description from the negative to the positive. If a couple's first answer to the miracle question is, "We wouldn't be fighting," the therapist can ask, "What would you be doing instead?"

. . . Must Be Concrete and Observable

I have been told by more than one client that I ask difficult questions, and it's true. I ask people to describe hard-to-describe things in terms that are observable and concrete. I ask them to express basic or generic ideas like *love* or *happiness* or *that feeling of excitement I had when we were dating* in specific personal terms. "Suppose you woke up tomorrow and you and your spouse were in love, what would that look like?"

Such questions aren't required in other approaches to therapy, so they may be unfamiliar to many practitioners, but they're tremendously helpful in solution-focused sessions. By the time a couple comes to therapy, they may be so preoccupied by their problem, the thought of what could be happening instead is unexplored territory. The answers the couple gives are often the first time one partner has heard the other talking about their behavior and their future in positive ways.

. . . Must Require Effort

It still shocks me to notice how much attention people pay to their problems and how little attention they pay to their successes. When people are asked how they fell in love, the typical answers are vague—"We just clicked" or "We just had amazing chemistry"—while their descriptions of problems are vivid and eloquent, as if they were reading the transcript of a recent argument aloud. If only human nature was the reverse, and we paid more attention to the details of our successes than we do to the symptoms of our problems, the world would be a happier place.

The role of a solution-focused marriage counselor is to remind couples of the process that was in play when they first fell in love, and what skills each partner brought to the relationship in its early days. When that process reboots and the skills that have been lying dormant reemerge, success becomes inevitable, and the world—for those couples at least—becomes a happier place.

. . . Must Be Created Equally by Both Partners

Earlier, I explained what I call SF tennis. This process of asking each partner the same question is to ensure that each partner contributes equally to the discussion. It's not to say that each partner needs to be given equal time—one partner may take 10 minutes answering a question, whereas the other can answer in just a few words. The important thing is that each partner takes a turn, so the conversation moves ahead in a direction acceptable to both members.

Details! You Can't Have Too Many

During an early trip to the BRIEF therapy practice in London, I watched Chris Iveson conduct a session with a young woman who had been struggling with a series of problem symptoms. As he worked with her to develop a picture of her preferred future, Iveson asked the miracle question. She answered by saying she'd wake up feeling happy instead of sad—a typically generic response. Iveson pressed for further details. "What time would it be?" The client looked puzzled. "About eight," she said. "Then what would you do," Iveson asked. "I'd walk to the bathroom." "As you climbed out of the bed on miracle day, which foot would hit the ground first?"

Why would Iveson be interested in the time of day? What was he hoping to learn with the question about the foot? He likely had no idea. He was simply probing for details—and the more details he got, the more complete the picture of the client's preferred future would be. Not all the details uncovered in this way will prove to be relevant or helpful, of course, but some will—and there's a way of telling in advance which will be which.

RACHEL AND RAY

Not long ago I met with an unmarried couple hoping to improve their relationship. They'd been living together for nearly 4 years. Ray was an entrepreneur who had started a successful hardware store, and Rachel was studying to become a nurse. It was clear on our first meeting that this couple was deeply in love with each other—I could sense it in every answer they gave to my early questions—so you can imagine my surprise when Rachel announced she'd recently moved out of the house she shared with Ray.

The problem was Ray's mother and her behavior toward Rachel. Rachel had grown up in a very close family and couldn't understand why Ray's mother was treating her so unfairly. Rachel's best efforts to get the mother's approval for her relationship with Ray had been met with only derision and insults. A recent argument had persuaded Rachel that the situation was hopeless. She felt that there was no chance that the mother would ever change, and the chances that Ray would ever stand up to his mother on her behalf were slim. Despite her love for Ray, she decided if she were to have a happy family life of her own, it couldn't be with him. Ray was devastated by Rachel's decision, but he seemed at least some-what relieved that he'd no longer be stuck in the middle between these two important women in his life.

I began the session with the best hopes question and Ray and Rachel had some trouble answering it. They both agreed that the mother was the problem and that the mother was standing in the way of their future plans. "How can we have children and build a happy life?," Rachel wondered. She wouldn't feel comfortable letting her children spend time with Ray's mother. Neither Rachel nor Ray could imagine their problem being solved because neither could envision the change in his mother's behavior.

I continued to pursue the best hopes answer, asking how they'd like their relationship to be working in the future. Finally, they were able to describe what they could see happening in their relationship *if* the mother changed her behavior in desirable ways. What the couple really wanted was to get married and build a family together.

This realization changed the dynamic of the conversation. They were now exploring only the interactions between the two of them and how they wanted their relationship to be different. The absence of the third party—Ray's mother—was no longer part of the discussion. As the ses-sion progressed, we amassed the details of the couple's preferred future.

I invited Ray and Rachel to make a list of 35 details they'd notice if their preferred future became a reality and prompted them with future-focused questions. The early details on the list tended to be vague or generic—they'd be closer, they'd be happier, and there would be more affection between them—but as we got farther along, the details grew richer, deeper, and more specific. The 28th entry came from Ray: "We would both realize that, no matter what my mother does or says, our love is stronger than her negativity."

When Rachel heard that, she reached out for Ray's hand and began to cry. "That's what I have been trying to get you to show me this whole time." As they talked about their love for each other, it was almost as if I was no longer in the room. They completed the list of 35 details and scheduled an appointment for the following week. There was a calmness about them as they strolled out of my office and into their "new" relationship.

Ray and Rachel had needed to talk through 27 different details of their future life until one of them hit on the detail that made all the difference. The session would likely not have been as successful for them if our list had stopped at 20 or even 25 details. I frequently make lists like this with my clients, as it usually takes dozens of answers to arrive at meaningful content.

THE "I DON'T KNOW" COUPLE

Brian and Leigh were a remarkable couple with a strong, successful history that needed to be rediscovered. They'd started dating in their second year of high school. It was a typical teenage romance in many ways. Their first date was at a water park, they talked on the phone until all hours of the night, and they went to the movies frequently. Then, barely a month into the relationship, Leigh discovered she was pregnant. It was devastating news for high school sophomores, and they turned to their families for advice. Leigh's angry parents insisted that she move out of their home. Brian's parents agreed to take Leigh in, and the couple decided to stay together and make the relationship work. After their child was born, Brian and Leigh enlisted the help of an aunt to watch the child during the school day, and they got jobs with flexible hours that ensured that one parent would always be available to care for the child when they were not in school. The couple decided to stop hanging out with their old friends, who were engaging in what they now considered to be risky behaviors. Brian and Leigh's list of accomplishments went on and on, and although times were tough for them, they made it through together and graduated.

In the years to come, the couple continued to grow. They both found full-time work. A second child was born. They eventually married and bought a house. Things seemed to be looking up. Then, for no apparent reason, Brian's disposition turned dark. Leigh noticed his unhappiness—and noticed too that she'd lost the ability to cheer him up or make him smile. For months, Leigh worked to understand what was wrong. What can I do? How can I help? She suggested counseling but Brian refused. He thought it was something he could get through on his own. Unfortunately, he was wrong. Weeks turned into months and the unhappiness lingered. Eventually, Brian agreed to seek help.

During my first session with Brian and Leigh, I asked them how they would know when their relationship had returned to its previous happy state. The couple was puzzled by this as well as other questions I was asking in trying to arrive at a preferred future description. The couple was trying to answer my questions, but simply couldn't. Again and again, "I don't know" was the best answer either of them could come up with.

Then at some point Brian finally said, "I guess I would remember what happiness looks like." This couple had grown up so fast and had been living like adults for so long, they'd forgotten how to have fun. This realization unlocked something for both partners, and the details of their preferred future began flooding out.

When the couple returned for their next session, they reported that, for the first time in their marriage, they were doing things for themselves. In looking back, the couple had realized that once they had children, they'd been so determined to create a life for the children that they'd forgotten how to relax and simply enjoy each other. In the week since the first session, Brian and Leigh hired a babysitter and went out twice, once to a pool hall and once to the movies. They rediscovered dating, something they'd done very little of in their lives together. In the coming weeks, the couple grew closer and closer. They were more affectionate, happier, even the children were behaving better. When I thought back to how many questions I had asked Brian and Leigh, and how many "I don't knows" I heard, this change was remarkable progress.

According to Chris Iveson (personal communication, July 1, 2009), when a client answers a question with "I don't know," it was either a dumb question or a question that the client has not thought of before. In the case of my early questions to Brian and Leigh, it was both. I needed to find the right way to ask them the questions, and they needed time to formulate their answers. Brian and Leigh knew what happiness looked like for them, but they'd forgotten all about it. I had to keep digging until they remembered.

SUMMARY

Eliciting a description of a couple's ideal future—without getting sucked into the problem story—is one of the hardest tasks in solution-focused therapy. This step requires that the therapist stay curious and thoroughly explore what the couple really wants, even if what they want is deeply hidden. Only when a preferred future is developed in enough detail, can the therapist move on the next phase of the session.

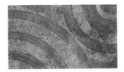

Step 5:
Scaling Toward the Preferred Future

"When I thought I couldn't go on, I forced myself to keep going.
My success is based on persistence, not luck."

—NORMAN LEAR

Scales are an important part of the solution-building process. They're indispensable in helping clients and therapists to track progress toward the preferred future, and they allow the client to play the expert role in evaluating that progress.

Here's an example of a scaling question:

Suppose, on a scale of zero to ten, we let ten represent the time when your preferred future becomes your new reality and zero is the time when you were as far away from that as possible. Where would you say you are today? Since no one is perfect and no one is a ten all the time, where do you think you will be on this scale when you realize that you no longer need therapy?

Here is how Michelle and Stephanie responded to the scaling question:

Therapist: I just have one more question. If on a scale of zero to ten, with ten representing a time when the kind of day you just described has become normal for you—when most of your days are like that day—and zero represents the opposite, when no days are like that day, where would you say you are today?

Michelle: [Laughing] I'm going to let Stephanie go first.

Therapist: It's okay, if you each have different answers.

Stephanie: Day-by-day, I would have to say that we are about a one, but the past week was a zero.

Therapist: Okay, Michelle, what would you say?

Michelle: I would say zero.

Therapist: Okay, thank you.

Because the couple had been so joyous in describing the details of their relationship when it was at its very best, this low rating seemed odd. In retrospect, I believe it indicated a strong desire to return to the best days of their relationship and their willingness to work toward that ideal. As we'll soon see, that's exactly what they did, with outstanding results.

Of all the skills a solution-focused therapist must master, scaling is one of the most challenging to explain. That's because scaling questions are uniquely flexible—they can be used at any point in the session to craft questions, develop next steps, or to shift the conversation away from problem talk toward solution talk. As I did in my conversation with Michelle and Stephanie, I most often ask the scaling question after a well-developed preferred future has been established, so that the answers can be used as a measurement toward that future.

Scaling questions are dynamic because they use the client's words and their description of their preferred future to move the conversation on to task development. This is in direct contrast to my early training as a counselor. At that time, I was working at a mental health agency that required all employees to use cognitive behavioral approaches in working with clients. That was a tremendous challenge to me because those problem-focused approaches weren't a good fit with my emerging solution-focused worldview. Another issue for me was the weekly staff meetings and group sessions in which the assembled clinicians developed tasks that were later assigned to individual clients. In my solution-focused world, the ideas for tasks and homework were coming from my clients and not from me or my colleagues. I was using scaling questions to help clients move beyond their problem toward a preferred future, and the reactions I was getting weren't the usual "I tried your suggestion and it didn't work," or, "I don't remember what we talked about during our last session." They were much more constructive than that. One day, my supervisor asked how I'd developed a particular effective task for a client family. I could only say, "It was their idea." For me, it had been a demonstration of the power and resources that clients have within themselves to develop their own ideas and reach their own goals, but I don't think my supervisor shared my enthusiasm.

In using scales or any other tool of solution-focused therapy properly, clinicians must trust our clients and their skills. At times, this may be contrary to our education and training, and I'll admit I wasn't an instant believer. It took working with and trusting my clients over the years and watching them develop far more effective interventions than anything I could have suggested. I credit my clients and couples for teaching me the most important lesson in solution-focused therapy—a simple belief in the process. Scales are part of the process, and they put the responsibility for assessing how things are, how things should be, and what steps can be taken to make things better right where they belong—in the hands of the clients themselves.

THE COMPONENTS OF A SCALE

There are four important points on a well-defined scale: the most-desired point, representing the preferred future (ten); the least-desired point (zero); the point representing where the couple is today; and the point representing where the couple will be when they realize there's no need for further therapy.

A Word About Ten

During my time at the mental health agency, I met a psychiatrist who used scales in his work. He suggested that his scales and the scales used in solution-focused therapy were the same, but he was wrong. He used scales to assess the severity of problems, as in, "How bad is the pain on a scale of zero to ten?" On his scale, ten is the very worst. Solution-focused practitioners use scales to chart a client's progress toward a desired future, to highlight exceptions, develop tasks, and identify strengths. On our scale, ten is the very best.

A Word About Zero

If clients give themselves a rating of zero, they're saying they feel they're as far from their preferred future as they can possibly be. It's important under those circumstances not to allow the problem to be reintroduced into the conversation. The more time spent defining zero, the more likely the couple will revert to problem talk, making solution building more difficult. Simply define zero as, "the opposite of ten," or "the time in your lives when you were as far from ten as possible," and leave it at that. In this situation—unlike virtually all other situations in solution-focused therapy—no details are needed.

Where the Couple Is Today

A critical part of developing a solution-focused scale is identifying the couple's current position on it. As seen in the session with Michelle and Stephanie, it's perfectly okay if the partners place themselves at different points on the scale. Couples often feel they should agree, and one partner may feel bad when rating the relationship lower than the other. The therapist should assure them it's not a problem—partners frequently experience problems differently and don't always feel the same level of unhappiness. The important thing is to have a starting point the therapist can use in crafting the questions to come.

Where They Would Like to Be

As no couple is perfect, reaching ten should not be the aim of therapy. Instead, set a more realistic target—where the couple will be when they realize the therapy has been successful. Solution-focused therapy begins with the endpoint in mind, and from the beginning, the practitioner should use termination language that will signal to the couple when further therapy is unnecessary.

Solution-focused therapy belongs to a larger category of proactive therapeutic approaches, collectively known as *brief therapy*. Brief therapies tend to be highly strategic and seek to accomplish a client's goal in the fewest number of sessions possible. Evan George may have said it best, "If we can accomplish the goal in one session, we should not take two. If the goal can be accomplished in 25 sessions, we should not take 26" (personal communication, June 20, 2011). We are seeking long-term improvements in a client's life, but we're working to accomplish it quickly.

SCALING EXAMPLES

There are so many uses for scaling questions, I will only highlight several of the most common ways to use them in a session.

Using Scales to Build Homework Tasks

Scales can be used to identify the steps that need to be taken by the couple, or each partner within the couple, to move the relationship closer to the desired outcome. This can be done by inviting the couple to answer questions about which role each of them could be playing. Here's an example from a real session:

Therapist: Let's let ten represent the time in the future *when* your relationship is at its very best, and let zero represent a time the two of you *were* as far away from that as possible. Where would you say you are today?

Husband: [To wife] I'll let you go first.

Wife: Okay, I would say we are a three or four.

Husband: I would say the same.

Therapist: Imagine for a moment that the two of you come back to my office next week and report that things have moved up the scale from three or four to a solid four or four point five. What changes would you each tell me that you must have made to allow this progress to occur?

69

You'll notice that I have highlighted the words *when* and *were* in the therapist's opening question. Those represent key presuppositions by the therapist. By asking the couple to look ahead to the time when their relationship will be ideal, instead of asking them if they could imagine such a time, the clinician is making the subtle but powerful assertion to the couple that progressive change is achievable. Similarly, by defining zero as the time when the partners *were* at their lowest point, instead of where they are now, the therapist is making another assumption and using the language to communicate it to the couple—the time when the couple was as far away from their desired future as possible was sometime in the past.

In this session, the couple answered the question immediately and began exploring what they could do in the future to move themselves higher on the scale. The wife promised to be kinder to her husband and to be more affectionate when they came home from work. The husband said he'd send text messages during the day to let his wife know he was thinking of her. He made another, more startling promise: he'd give his wife the passwords to his e-mail accounts, cell phone, and social media sites. That was a significant development, because it had been discovered that he was having an affair with an old friend he'd reconnected with on Facebook. The husband had been refusing to give his wife the password information for weeks—they'd even had an argument about it at the beginning of our session. Now, less than an hour later, he'd had a change of heart. What triggered it? I can only report that in the course of solution-focused therapy, people sometimes make decisions for themselves that could otherwise not have been forced on them by anyone.

In this case, both the husband and the wife followed through on the promises they made in the session, and over the next few months, they would successfully rebuild their relationship.

Using Scales to Identify a Couple's Strengths

Identifying strengths is another way to pivot the conversation toward helpful information that can be used to create lasting change. When couples are asked to identify the traits and skills that have helped to build their relationship, they're often unable to express any specific examples of what made the relationship successful. "I don't know, we just clicked," is a typical answer. Scaling questions can help the couple get in touch with what they did or are doing well, so that those successes can be repeated.

Sara and Michael came to see me after a very hurtful event that had caused significant trust issues between them. At the beginning of the session, when asked what the two liked about each other, they weren't able to offer many details. After the scaling question, their recollections improved greatly.

Michael: It is funny, since we made this appointment things have been a bit better.

Sara: Yeah, that is true.

Therapist: How much better have things been? On a scale from zero to ten, if ten represents a time in your future when your relationship is at its very best, and zero represents a point in your past before scheduling the appointment, where are you now?

Michael: I would say we are at a three or four now. Things have been tough lately.

Sara: I was going to say we are at a two or three.

Therapist: What if I had asked the two of you to rate your relationship on that same scale before your decision to make the appointment?

Michael and Sara: [Simultaneously] Zero.

Sara: Yeah, zero for sure, we were not at all doing well.

This use of the scaling question allowed the couple to begin exploring the progress they'd already made, instead of rehashing the problem. The session moved directly toward helpful information. After spending some time examining the signs of progress they'd noticed, another scaling question was used.

Therapist: So, I am curious, what skills did the two of you use to move yourselves up the scale as far as you did?

Michael: Not sure. We were definitely communicating a bit better and being more affectionate. It is not like everything was better, but we were definitely talking more and being more affectionate.

Therapist: Sara, what about you? What skills did you use to help the relationship move further up the scale?

Sara: [Pause] I was caring and forgiving. Knowing we had this session scheduled helped me relax because I knew if anything bothered me, I could wait and bring it up here.

Therapist: I see, so that allowed your caring and forgiving nature to become a bigger part of your relationship.

Sara: Yes.

Therapist: What else?

Michael: I was more patient and a better listener.

Therapist: How different is this, for you to be patient and a good listener in recent weeks?

Michael: Very different. I admit I have not been the best husband lately.

Therapist: Let's suppose that tomorrow the two of you wake up in a world when these positive traits you just discussed, and many others we did not discuss, were playing an even bigger role in your relationship than they did this past week. What will each of you begin to notice?

For the rest of the session, the couple explored what the changes would look like as they moved closer toward their preferred future. In the coming weeks, the couple eventually felt that they had accomplished their goals for the treatment, and if needed they could come in every 6 weeks or so to ensure the changes were being sustained. After only a few more visits, it was clear to all involved that continued therapy was not needed. The couple's confidence in themselves had blossomed. Scaling had helped Michael and Sara crystallize their progress by increasing their ability to identify the skills that enabled it.

Using Scales to Identify Exceptions

As we've learned, exceptions (de Shazer et al., 2007) are things a couple does despite a problem without consciously knowing they are doing them. Because exceptions are done without knowledge or intent, people can be completely unaware of them. Scaling questions like these can bring exceptions to light, so that they can be understood and repeated:

- On a scale from zero to ten, when in the past few weeks were the two of you closest to ten?

- Even if it only lasted for a brief time, what did it look like? What were you doing?

- What did you notice your partner was doing during those times when the problem was not present?

Such questions encourage couples to uncover hidden assets in their relationship and behaviors that have been occurring without their awareness. By realizing that the problem plaguing them is not *always* present, they begin to understand that it's possible to replicate their exceptions.

There's another positive aspect to uncovering exceptions. In discussing times in the recent past when the couple behaved as if the problem did not exist, partners often become considerate of each other. That often breaks the problem pattern that has been bedeviling their relationship and the conversations between them. The language of exceptions is almost always complimentary, and frequently, it's the first exchange of loving words between the partners in some time.

SUMMARY

Scaling questions are a dynamic and flexible tool the therapist can use in a variety of ways to engage couples in the solution-building process. They help the therapist build on the couple's own words and worldview in moving the conversation forward. In solution building, the couple themselves are the greatest asset, and scaling questions are a valuable source of insights into the strengths and resources the couple has within them.

Step 6:
Wrapping Up

Taking a Break, Providing Feedback, and Making Suggestions

"We shall neither fail nor falter; we shall not weaken or tire . . . give us the tools and we will finish the job."

—Winston Churchill

I had a professor who taught me that the most important parts of a session are the first few minutes and the last few minutes. The beginning of the session establishes the foundation for the solution-building process and the closing session solidifies it. The first task of a session is to establish what the end will look like—getting a clear idea of the preferred future the couple will work toward in therapy. At the end of the conversation, the task is to offer feedback and suggestions that will help the couple move in the right direction.

Before giving feedback to Michelle and Stephanie, I took a break:

Therapist: I'd like to share a few things that have stood out to me as we talked here today. There was a lot that was going through my mind as we talked, so I'd like to take a short break to collect my thoughts and make a few notes, if that's okay with you guys.

Stephanie: Sure, that's fine.

Michelle: Okay.

I don't take notes during my sessions, so I take a brief break to gather my thoughts and write down on index cards the strengths, assets, and successes I've been hearing. While Michelle and Stephanie chatted with each other, I spent about 5 minutes recalling the things about this couple that made their relationship work well. I recalled how they'd begun to build their relationship on that first night in the bar, and I made a list of their strengths and successes using Michelle and Stephanie's own words from the session.

Therapist: Okay, thanks for giving me a few minutes to get my thoughts together, that's very helpful for me and I appreciate it. I have a few things I would like to share with the two of you. Can I start with you, Michelle?

Michelle: Sure.

Therapist: Okay, thanks. Michelle, what stands out to me most about you is that you are such a strong and passionate person. Several times in our conversation, you used examples in the past about being passionate, wanting a kiss, wanting to be touched. That seemed to play a big role in the strength of the relationship between the two of you in the early days. You also seem to be a great communicator. From the night you guys met, you were very direct and confident, and you made sure that you and Stephanie would talk. Even here today, you're very clear in the way you express yourself. It made my talking with you much easier, and I'll bet when things are working between the two of you, it makes it easier for Stephanie to be in the relationship with you. Does that all make sense?

Michelle: [Wiping away tears] Yes, that makes perfect sense, that is so right. When things are working between the two of us, I'm able to be myself and she gets me.

Therapist: Stephanie, you seem to be a very stable and patient person. Michelle's great passion is balanced by your great stability.

Stephanie: Yeah, I'm very laid back and reserved.

Therapist: Yes very, and it was that quiet swagger that made her notice you originally. It still seems to be a part of who you are.

Michelle: Yes, it's still there. [She reaches for Stephanie's hand.]

Therapist: I enjoyed observing each of your strengths, and it seems that each of you is able to make the other happy just by using the strengths you possess. I was able to see that during the session.

Stephanie: [Now holding hands] Thank you.

Michelle: Yes, thank you so much.

Therapist: I guess we are out of time. Before you leave, can I ask you what we accomplished here today?

Michelle: I was able to realize that I really do want to be with Stephanie. You didn't know this, but I've been involved with my ex lately, and I came to this session very confused. I wasn't sure what I wanted. Things have been so bad between Stephanie and me that I let someone else in. Sitting here listening to her talk about me and listening to your questions made me realize that this is where I want to be.

Stephanie: I am just so hopeful hearing that, that is what I wanted to accomplish with this session. I am leaving here with hope.

Therapist: That is so great to hear. It was a pleasure meeting with both of you. If you think it would be helpful, I'd be happy to meet with you again in the next week or two.

Stephanie: Sure.

Michelle: I would like that.

Therapist: Until then, would you guys look for signs that things are improving between the two of you? Just try to catch even the smallest clues that things are improving between now and the next session.

Michelle: Yes, I can do that.

Stephanie: Me too.

The session ended with the couple scheduling their next session.

Throughout most of the session, I was asking questions to draw out the details of Michelle and Stephanie's preferred future. Now at the end, my task was to amplify the strengths and positive traits that were identified in the conversation, so for the first time in the session, I was doing more talking than they were. The list of compliments I give them at the end of a session often becomes the very data they'll use to transform their relationship into a more desirable experience.

THE BREAK

My first experience in using a break came when I was in graduate school. One of my fellow students was having a hard time helping a couple move past their problems. The professor suggested that our class of about eight students act as a reflection team to generate new ideas. We watched a live session with the problem couple from an observation room with a two-way mirror. The professor, a solution-focused practitioner, instructed us to watch the couple for signs of strengths and resources, and the student therapist was instructed to take a break toward the end of the session to meet with us for feedback. Many different approaches to psychotherapy use breaks and reflection teams in working with individuals and couples, but this was the first time I was playing a role.

We sat with the student therapist during the break, listing the positive things about that couple that we'd noticed and the compliments we thought he should share with them. He returned to the session room and simply read the list. I was stunned to see the couple's reaction. They became tearful and held hands as they listened, and when it was over, all they could say was, "wow."

The next time this couple came to the university clinic, they reported that they'd had one of the best weeks of their relationship and were looking forward to many more weeks like it. No homework had been assigned to them in the first session, and the student therapist had offered them no profound insights. He'd only read them a list of compliments, but that had had a simple and powerful effect.

Reflection teams play an important role in solution-focused therapy at the Brief Family Therapy Center in Milwaukee (de Shazer et al., 2007), but by taking a break to develop well thought-out compliments and suggestions for a couple, individual therapists can act as their own reflection teams.

GIVING FEEDBACK

Using the couple's own words is the most important step in formulating helpful feedback. It requires that the therapist pay close attention to the language used throughout the conversation and to stick with it.

At one of my early jobs, I was required to take notes during sessions and complete extensive client assessments later on. Using the diagnostic thinking and assessment tools associated with the problem-focused model favored by my agency, I was expected to develop interventions and homework tasks that would supposedly help my clients achieve their goals. I found this difficult. I've never thought of myself as having any special knowledge that puts me in a position to teach others how to live better lives. Very often, when I, or the treatment team that I was part of, developed a homework task for a particular client, the client's response would be, "I've already tried that and it didn't work," or, "That won't work for us because. . . ." If clients refused a homework task, or if the task proved ineffective, it was common for the supervisors at my agency to label those clients "resistant." That's when I began to understand the differences between solution-focused therapy and problem-focused approaches. There's nothing wrong with problem-focused therapies, and I'm not suggesting they cannot be effective. But because focusing on a client's description of their preferred future made better sense to me, I began working with my clients from that perspective.

Once I changed my emphasis, I saw an immediate change in the way the clients, families, and couples responded to feedback. Clients were no longer telling me that they couldn't complete their homework assignment or that they didn't remember what was said in the previous session. Instead, they came to therapy more eager to report the progress they'd noticed by doing the tasks they'd developed for themselves. Surprisingly, clients began to ask me for the note cards I used to list their strengths, resources, and successes. When I was practicing from a problem-focused perspective, no one had ever asked me for my notes— not once. Now, it was happening several times per week. Couples, adolescents, adults, males, and females were all asking me for my note cards. Why? My hypothesis is that when I started using the actual language my clients were using, my feedback made more sense to them. It became more meaningful and memorable. In my previous work, it was as if I were trying to persuade my clients to buy into a reality they didn't recognize or understand. What I believe now is, if you do not accept the client's worldview and language, if you don't develop tasks based on their perception of reality, the therapy will have little chance of being effective.

Feedback should be related to the couple's strengths and the traits that have the potential to lead them away from their problem toward the preferred future. This is not the time to offer opinions about what the couple should be doing differently, or to teach them what they could be doing to fix their problem. The therapist is *not* an expert in the couple's lives. The solution-building process requires a therapist to offer nothing more than an amplification of a couple's strengths and resources using their own words. Once the couple is aware of their strengths and reminded of their past successes, once they realize their successes did not occur by accident, they become more able to resolve the issues that brought them into therapy without further intervention by the therapist. The answer truly does reside within the client.

MAKING SUGGESTIONS

In early family therapy literature (Haley, 1984, 1986; Minuchin, 1974) as well as early solution-focused literature (de Shazer, 1985, 1988; Walter & Peller, 1992), making suggestions and invitations was referred to as assigning tasks. The newer language seems more accurate. Solution-focused practitioners don't develop tasks in the same way that problem-focused practitioners do. They simply use the couple's language in inviting them to use their strengths, or in suggesting that they do more of something that seems to be working. Often, the suggestion is to simply notice what has gotten better between appointments.

The human urge to help people "solve" their problem is strong, and it often tempts practitioners to "teach" couples how to be more successful. Resist the urge. A couple's strengths can be amplified without any interference from the therapist, and certainly without imposing unfamiliar ideas on them.

When couples come to therapy, they are typically seeking to improve their relationship by improving communication between the partners. They'll say, "We can't communicate," or, "We never agree." It can be tempting to give them lessons on eye contact or "I" statements or other basics of effective communication. Instead, we can invite them to notice that, in deciding to come to therapy, choosing a therapist, and showing up for their appointment, the couple elected to try something different rather than "obeying" their problem. If they disobeyed their problem to accomplish that, they may also be disobeying their problem at other times without noticing it. There may be times when they simply forget they have a problem and temporarily get on with their relationship in a healthier way. When we invite couples to pay more attention to the exceptions in their lives, their ability to create other exceptions increases. They often realize that they've been more successful than they've given themselves credit for. At that point, ideas for further progress can be generated by the couple, for the couple, and drawing on the couple's best traits. This drastically increases compliance and follow-through. I cannot count the number of times I've come up with an idea that struck my mind for a couple during a session, but I wisely shut my mouth as they came up with a far better plan all by themselves.

SUMMARY

Wrapping up a solution-building session is about trusting the clients and trusting the process. The person who first exposed me to the ideas of solution-focused therapy was Dr. Linda Metcalf, a former professor who's now my close friend. In those days, I was so skeptical that solution-focused therapy could be as simple as it seemed, and I spent hours badgering Linda with questions about the approach, looking for evidence that it does, in fact, work. Ultimately, proof came from the couples, families, and individuals I saw in my practice. They told me over and over again that their lives were improving, that our sessions were giving them hope, and allowing them to move forward. Many of my clients had previously seen other therapists with little progress to show for it. In time, couples were coming to my office from miles around because they'd heard that I was the guy who asked the strange questions that worked. I experimented with solution-focused therapy because it made sense to me on a theoretical level, but I became addicted to it because it works.

For the past few years of my practice, I've been seeing more than 25 couples a week and I'm still amazed by the progress I see and the love stories I hear. I cannot say that solution-focused therapy will help every couple or save every marriage. I can only say that I trust the process to unlock the solutions I know clients have within them.

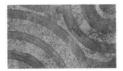

Follow-Up Sessions

What to Do After the First Meeting

"Action is the foundational key to all success."
—PABLO PICASSO

A criticism I often hear from students of solution-focused therapy (SFT) is that the training materials are generally drawn only from the first session. When I conduct trainings, many people ask me about second sessions and beyond. It happens so frequently. In fact, I decided early on to include a chapter about follow-up sessions in planning this project. The first session is the critical one, and in SFT, it's sometimes the only one. However, many couples will come to therapy more than once, so a practitioner must be ready to ensure that subsequent sessions continue to move the couple in the direction of their preferred future.

The procedure for follow-up sessions isn't dissimilar from that of first sessions except that the steps are followed in a slightly different order. Since a direction was established in the first session, the second session begins by assessing progress toward that direction and builds from there. The second session is more flexible than the first because much of the content depends on what has happened between the sessions.

The second session occurs in four steps, which I'll illustrate with transcripts of my recent sessions with Carl and Geri. They'd decided to seek therapy because, after 25 years of marriage, Geri's husband had discovered that she was having an affair with her personal trainer.

When I asked the best hopes question in the first session, Carl said he just wanted to get their relationship back to the time when he thought that he and Geri were perfect for each other. Through tears, he detailed how his life had been changed by her violation of his trust. I asked him how he would know that he and Geri were getting back to a time when they were perfect for each other, and he said he'd be affectionate again and able to talk to Geri about their relationship.

When I asked Geri what her best hopes from this meeting would be, she became very emotional. She said she regretted her actions and that she had never meant to hurt Carl. She reached out for her husband's hand, and as they held hands, she said that she too wanted things to be the way they used to be. When asked to describe what she meant, Geri said that she hoped Carl could trust her again and the two of them could be as close and in love as they were earlier.

As the session moved on, we worked together to explore the couple's successful past, developed a picture of the preferred future, scaled their distance from their preferred future—the couple felt they were between two and three—and reviewed the feedback and suggestions. As the session ended, the couple agreed to notice all the signs that things were moving toward their preferred future and off they went.

FOLLOW-UP STEP 1:
IDENTIFY SIGNS OF PROGRESS

It's often surprising to see what happens to couples between sessions—partners on the verge of divorce sometimes return as lovebirds. It's my clients who've taught me to believe in SFT, and witnessing the progress between first and second sessions has been a big part of that learning.

The therapist begins the second session by asking, "What has been better?" This communicates an assumption of progress on the part of the therapist and allows the solution-building process begun in the first session to continue. Asking about what has been better—as opposed to "How have things been?" or "How are you doing?"—moves the couple away from problem language that might counteract the progress made up to that point. It's very important to understand that the follow-up session starts with the progress between sessions—even if the clients have a hard time identifying any evidence of progress. De Jong and Berg, in their book *Interviewing for Solutions* (2008), point out that this can be a difficult concept for students of SFT to grasp. Many times, the assumption is that we will begin by asking whether suggestions made in the earlier session were accomplished by the couple or simply by asking, "How are things going?" In SFT, the assumption is that the clients either completed the suggestion or did something that worked even better. By asking, "What has been better?" we convey a sense of confidence in the couple and their ability to solve the problem. If we were to ask, "Is anything better?" the couple might take it to mean that the therapist had some doubt about what they may have been able to accomplish.

By first asking about what has been better, the couple gets another message: what they do well is more important than what they do not do well. This is a crucial idea in solution building. The skills and traits that people use to make progress are the foundation for more progress; so, these positives must be uncovered and examined. A couple may not notice just how much progress they've made until they are directly questioned about it. They may come to the session thinking that not much has improved, but when asked about the things they did well between sessions, they'll begin to reveal positive details that have not been top of mind. Once one of the partners recalls a positive detail, other details will follow more easily.

A question that the workshop attendees often ask about SFT is what to do if a couple brings up a problem or reports that things have not improved. When couples bring up problem data, it's important for the therapist to acknowledge the problem without being overly curious about the details of it at that point—the problem will be resolved later in the solution-building process.

In working with Carl and Geri, this is how the solution building that was begun in the first session continued in the second session:

Therapist: So, what has gotten better since we met last week?

Carl: I don't think anything got too much better.

Geri: Yeah, there were some rough moments.

Therapist: I am sure there were, but what got even just a little bit better?

[A long pause and much shrugging of shoulders.]

Therapist: Suppose there had been a reality TV show crew following the two of you during the past week, filming you every minute of every day. When we watched that footage, what signs would there have been that some things had gotten better, even though there were rough moments?

Geri: He was nicer to me at times.

Therapist: What would that look like on the video?

Geri: He held me as we slept a few nights and we were able to talk without fighting at times.

Therapist: Oh really, when were those times?

Geri: The other night we went for a walk around the neighborhood.

Therapist: Whose idea was that?

Carl: It was mine. It was a nice night and she mentioned wanting to take more walks together, so I figured it would be a good time.

Therapist: If the camera crew captured that moment, what would they have caught the two of you doing on this walk?

Geri: Nothing much, walking, talking, holding hands, you know, stuff like that.

Therapist: What did you do to ensure the conversation didn't turn into an argument?

Carl: It was just such a nice evening. We just talked about the things we were noticing in the neighborhood. The trees were starting to bloom and people had flowers in their front yards that were blooming.

Geri: Yeah, it was a lot of fun. It was a very pleasant walk. Looking back, it was nice to spend time not talking about the same old problem. Too bad it didn't last all week.

Therapist: Yeah, that is too bad, how long did it last though?

Carl: I think we were gone for about 30 minutes. Not too long but it was still very nice.

Therapist: Is there anything else the video footage would show going well between the two of you since our last session?

Carl: Yeah, we were intimate a couple of times; it was good I thought. [Looks to Geri]

Geri: Yes, I thought so too.

Therapist: Did that come as a surprise to the two of you?

Geri: Yes, he has been so mad at me that he has barely touched me recently. It was nice for him to show me he still loves me. I was starting to doubt it, to be honest.

Carl: She even instigated it once.

There are a few things about this dialogue I'd like to point out. First, there had been clear signs of progress, even though the couple wasn't able to recall any of the instances when first asked. The therapist's task is to keep digging for positives. Next, it would be too impossible for *something* not to have gotten at least a little bit better—even if other things got much worse. In the case of Carl and Geri, they had some difficult moments that week, and that's what was on their minds while coming into the session. They weren't fully aware of the things that had actually gone well. By digging a bit and rephrasing the question, I was able to open a pathway to the sign of progress that had indeed occurred between them. In their case, the progress was significant, and that helped them uncover more details as they talked further. In the end, they managed to remember several positive aspects of their week despite the rough moments.

Something else I would highlight in this exchange is the therapist's handling of the couple's report that nothing had improved, and the problem language that came up later in the excerpt. The therapist's task is to accept the reality that the couple is reporting, and not to challenge or ignore it. Even though we must maintain the belief that something has gotten better, we can't reject the couple's answer if they say otherwise. You'll notice I responded to Carl and Geri by clearly saying I understood they were reporting that something difficult had happened, but that I was asking them to focus on something else for the time being. That's very different from saying, "But surely something must have gotten better." If I'd said that, the couple might have tried persuading me that they were right and I was wrong—that, in fact, nothing had gotten better. That's the opposite direction in which I want to take them. I want them to describe the good moments, so I asked the same question in a different way. I believed that something must have improved. It's very hard to have a week where everything goes wrong—there must have been *something* that was better, even if it was a small thing or only slightly better. That's the data I'm interested in—information that can be used to build solutions that enable the couple's preferred future.

FOLLOW-UP STEP 2: AMPLIFYING THE SIGNS OF PROGRESS

Several years ago, I worked with a couple who taught me the importance of amplifying the signs of progress. Tony and Gail were in their mid-forties and came to therapy because of her concerns about his drinking. Tony acknowledged drinking more than 25 shots of whiskey a day and spending much of his time in three neighborhood bars. He'd built a successful insurance business years ago but had lost it because of his drinking problem. He'd racked up a number of DWI (driving while intoxicated) arrests and faced a lengthy prison sentence if it happened again. The couple was living on the residual income from his business, which barely covered the household expenses and his bar tabs. When asked what had been better in the week following their first session, Tony became upset and reported that he hadn't been able to stop drinking—not even for a single day, as he'd promised Gail he would. He broke down as he admitted he'd been drinking every day and that he'd even driven on several of those days. But that wasn't the whole picture. After a few more questions, he mentioned that on one of the days, he had less to drink than usual. When asked why he thought that happened, he had an interesting response. He said that on that particular day, he'd run out of clean clothes and had to put on a business suit for the first time in years. How did that make a difference? He said it made him feel more professional. It raised his self-esteem. As a consequence, he spent more of his time in the bars talking and less time drinking. He'd met new people. He knew he had less to drink that night because he'd managed to come home with money in his pocket. As an experiment, Tony agreed to wear his professional clothes more often to see if he would continue to drink less.

In the following weeks, the drinking diminished significantly. Other things in his life began to change as well. His relationship with his children improved. He stopped seeing his mistress. He and Gail grew closer. After several increasingly good weeks, Gail came to our scheduled session without him. She told me she'd come home one evening to find Tony packing his bags—he wanted her to drive him to a local hospital for rehabilitation. After years of resisting the idea, and ignoring her threats to leave him because of it, he finally decided to get himself off alcohol safely and for good.

I had no idea what led Tony to make this change and neither did Gail. Still I can't help but wonder if this would have happened if we hadn't noticed the connection between the drinking and Tony's feelings of low self-esteem. He never noticed any pattern to his drinking and felt he had no power to control it. Then by noticing and amplifying a positive change, he gained a sense of power that eventually led him to remove alcohol from his life.

A little over 2 years after working with the couple, I received a letter from Tony. He wrote that he'd been sober for 18 months and was now coaching his son's baseball team. He sent me a pin showing that the team won a recent tournament. I kept that pin in my office to remind me that even when the situation seems bleak, the solution is always within the client. We just have to believe.

Amplifying signs of progress with couples can be as simple as asking, "How did you notice that?," or, "Did you notice your wife was happy when you_____?," or, "Are you surprised now to hear your husband say how much that hug meant to him?" Often, the miracle moments happen when we aren't looking for them, so we're unaware of them in real time. By examining these moments later in the session, clients begin to see that such moments don't happen randomly or by coincidence—they occur because of specific actions that can be repeated.

Highlighting the skills used to create progress also helps with amplification. By asking "What skill did you use to_____?," or, "What was it about you that allowed you to_____?," the couple can begin to recognize the specific traits and positive attributes that led to their successes. Those positive traits can then be amplified to enable further steps toward the preferred future.

Below is the part of my second session with Carl and Geri where we began to amplify the changes they'd made in the previous week.

Therapist: At what point did the two of you realize you were going to have a better week?

Carl: [Laughing] Today!

Geri: Yeah, I don't think either of us realized how many good signs there were.

Therapist: Now that we are looking back, how did you guys do it? I guess what I am asking is what allowed you to make such progress?

Carl: I think we really love each other and that love is stronger, maybe, than we both thought.

Therapist: Wow, that's very interesting. You believe it is your strong love that allowed progress to happen. Geri, what do you think it was?

Geri: I have to agree, I made a horrible mistake [in having an affair] and I wish I could take it back, but I love him very much and hope to show him that more and more.

Therapist: It seems to be showing this week.

As the conversation went on, they continued to uncover traits and characteristics that they believed led them to have a better week, and as they did so, they stopped bringing up the problem they'd mentioned earlier in the session. This is not uncommon. When couples begin to explore the details of progress and talk about the skills they possess that led to the progress, it is almost as if they are complimenting each other for the way they behaved between sessions. This may be the first time they've talked about their relationship in positive terms in quite some time, and the effect of that can be profound.

FOLLOW-UP STEP 3:
WHERE ARE YOU ON THE
SCALE NOW?

Now that we've spent some time uncovering the signs that things have gotten better, and examined how the couple was able to make those changes happen, we can return to our scale once again. The scale in the follow-up session is used exactly the way it was used in the first session.

I'm always stunned that so many couples remember how they ranked themselves in the earlier session. Time after time, people get it exactly right, which simplifies the task of monitoring progress. But if a couple can't remember their ranking, simply ask them, "Looking back, where would you have ranked yourselves in that first session?" This gives the couple a basis for comparison in the second session.

Another point to make about the scale: it's okay if each partner rates themselves at different points. One person may have experienced the week more positively than the other because of some circumstance or another. In my experience, this is rare, since in relationships (even troubled ones), as one person improves, the other usually does as well. But remember, the scale is about measuring progress using the couple's own language and worldview, so it doesn't matter where they are on the scale as long as the therapist gets the data needed to build questions. Solution building is about composing the next question while adhering to the couple's language and worldview as closely as possible. Scales are an important part of solution building because they allow the clinician to assess the effectiveness of the work being done in concert with the couple themselves. There's no need for the clinician to assume the role of the expert in accessing effectiveness—that would only make subsequent solution building more difficult.

In the follow-up session with Carl and Geri, this is how the scaling question was used:

Therapist: So, after a week, when so many things showed signs of improvement, where would the two of you rank yourselves on the scale? Do you remember the scale from the first session? Ten is you at your best and zero is the opposite.

Carl: Yes, I think I said I was at a one, it was pretty low.

Geri: I think I said three.

Therapist: Where would you rank yourselves today?

Geri: You go first. [Looking at Carl]

Carl: I would say five. We still have a long way to go, but we're getting there.

Geri: That's what I was going to say—five.

Therapist: Wow, so things have gotten much better.

Something to point out here is that the scale question was asked after the couple had reviewed the progress of the previous week. That's important. If the question had been asked earlier, the couple might not have answered it with success on their minds. They might still been thinking about the problem they brought with them to the session, and their answer would likely have been filled with problem-saturated language. By taking a few minutes to dig for signs of progress toward the preferred future, the therapist increases the likelihood that the couple's answer to the scaling question will contain useful solution-building data.

What If Things Have Not Gotten Better?

There are times when a couple will report that nothing has gotten better, and further questions won't uncover any examples of improvement. Although such times are rare, it's important for the clinician to know how to handle them. Even if a couple says things have stayed the same, it's still something that can be amplified using the usual process. "How did you prevent things from getting worse?," "What skills did you use?" These questions and others like them shift the focus from blaming them for not *progressing*, which would likely cause the couple to feel worse about their situation, to giving them credit for not *declining* what is likely to make them feel better.

In cases when the couple states that things are worse, it's more important than ever for the therapist to shift the focus away from problem-saturated language to a language that can be more useful. For example, if the couple says things have been worse, the question would be, "How did the two of you cope with things getting worse?," or, "What skills did you use to cope with that situation?" These questions continue to give credit to the couple and honor their efforts to deal with the issue. This is appropriate and valuable—even if the only overt evidence of progress is that they came to a follow-up session together.

FOLLOW-UP STEP 4: ADVANCING THE PREFERRED FUTURE

Just as in the first session, this follow-up step is about moving the conversation into the future by asking future-focused questions. The scale answer is an important part of the shift because it keeps the language focused on what is doable and realistic.

When I was a child, my father took me to a restaurant in Boston that was known for serving hamburgers the size of a dinner plate. In my childish naiveté, I was certain I could handle one of these monsters, but when it arrived I complained to my father that it was too big—I couldn't possibly finish it. My father reached over and cut my hamburger into eight pieces. Suddenly the meal looked manageable, and I dug right in.

Step 4 takes the preferred future established in the first session and breaks it down into smaller, more achievable pieces. This is done by asking the couple to imagine what might improve in the week ahead and listening for the details they identify. Here is how the question was asked in the session with Carl and Geri:

Therapist: Imagine for a minute that somehow, as you leave here today, the positive parts of yourselves and the love in your relationship will play an even bigger role in your lives—so much so you'll move up a full point on the scale from five to six. How would the two of you notice that?

Geri and Carl began to describe a world where they were taking more walks, holding hands more often, and being more loving. They began to hold hands in the session, and the more they described this future

93

world, the closer they became right there in front of me. The majority of a follow-up session is spent exploring such details, because they hold the greatest potential in opening pathways to positive change.

FOLLOW-UP STEP 5:
FEEDBACK AND SUGGESTIONS

There is literally no difference between the way this is done in the first session and follow-up sessions, although I've noticed I'm less likely to take a break before delivering feedback in follow-up sessions. The more time I spend with the couple, the more their strengths and successes become apparent to me—I need less time to put together my list of compliments and evidence of success. My feedback for Carl and Geri was that I felt their love must be quite strong for them to have a week with so much progress despite the difficulties. I complimented both partners on the skills they'd used to create the progress, and I asked them to notice signs that progress was continuing in the coming week.

One More Thing About Suggestions

Couples very often uncover signs of the progress they're making in the process of complimenting one another, so it's not uncommon for me to suggest they continue complimenting each other in the time between sessions. This invites the couple to bring positive conversations back into their lives as well as in the sessions.

SUMMARY

Now that we have reviewed a first session and a follow-up session and detailed the steps in the solution-building process, I hope I've accomplished my goal of demonstrating how to build solution-focused conversations with couples. Arming a couple with an awareness of their own best traits, and sending them out into the world on a pathway toward their preferred future, is deeply rewarding—an experience that never gets old. When you trust your clients and rely on the skills and abilities they bring into the session, the ideas they leave with are powerful indeed.

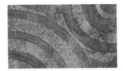

The Questions

Building Questions That Lead to Meaningful Responses

*"I think, at a child's birth, if a mother could ask a fairy godmother to
endow it with the most useful gift, that gift should be curiosity."*
—ELEANOR ROOSEVELT

When I was a graduate student, I read a number of books about different
therapeutic methodologies, many of which argued the merits of their particular approaches in theoretical terms. My goal in writing this book wasn't
to explain how or why solution-focused therapy (SFT) works, but instead
I simply wanted only to explain what actually happens in sessions with
solution-focused (SF) therapists and their clients. I wanted to demonstrate
how SF conversations with couples are constructed. I wanted to outline
the different steps of solution building and to highlight the tasks of the
therapist at every step.

At workshops, I'm frequently asked, "How did you know to ask that
question?" My answer is always that the questions come from the client's
previous response. Everything that's said in a session contributes to what
comes next—what the clients say contributes to what I ask, and what I ask
contributes to their response. Just as a client cannot answer my question
until I ask it, I cannot ask the next question until they've answered the
previous one.

This chapter is a review of the questions that are frequently asked in SFT and how they can be used with couples. We've briefly discussed the miracle question, the scaling question, and exception-finding questions, many of which have been written about extensively over the years. Now I'd like to share some of the questions I used in my practice that I found to be helpful in generating meaningful responses from couples.

DEVELOPING QUESTIONS

SF questions spring from a therapist's curiosity—curiosity is the foundation of solution building. The therapist listens to a couple's responses and decides what to be curious about in building the next question. When I'm training students and other therapists, I'm sometimes asked how I'd handle some particularly difficult situation or another. I can't answer such questions. I cannot know what I'd ask a client, or how I'd phrase the question, until the client has given me data and language to work with. The only questions I know in advance that I'll ask are, first, "What are your best hopes for this conversation?" and, second, "How did you two meet?"

I've said that SFT with couples requires trust. One has to trust the clients' answers—and use their own language—to build the next question. Look again at this, an example from the session with Michelle and Stephanie:

Therapist: So, Stephanie, since you are the first one to wake, what would first give you the idea that something was different?

Stephanie: About her or about me?

Therapist: Either.

Stephanie: Well, probably she would wake up and say good-bye or I love you [when I left for work] or something like that.

Therapist: What would be different about the way she said good-bye or I love you on this day compared to other days when she has said similar things?

Stephanie: It would be an extra minute longer, a deeper kiss.

As I asked Stephanie about the clues she would notice when the problem is gone, I was curious about the smallest details. She said Michelle would say either, "I love you," or, "good-bye," or, "something like that," as Stephanie left for work. I could have been curious about any part of that response. I could have explored "I love you" or "good-bye" or asked her to define "something like that." Instead, I asked about "I love you" as well as "good-bye," constructing a question that used Stephanie's exact words.

Was that the right choice? In the moment before hearing the client's response, the therapist has no way of knowing. If the response is useful and leads to further detail, then it was the right choice. If not, a new question needs to be developed. In this case, Stephanie answered with more details of a morning when the problem was not present and that led to many more useful responses. But I had no way of knowing in advance that that's what would happen. I was simply curious. Stephanie might have responded in a less helpful way, and I would have had to develop a new question to get the information I needed.

INVITING COUPLES TO DISCUSS
THEIR BEST

There are times that answering questions about what's right for a couple is difficult for them. Perhaps, it's been so long since they knew happier times that no positive details of those days come to mind. Maybe something hurtful has happened recently that's put one partner in a negative frame of mind. Or perhaps the relationship is in such disrepair that the couple honestly believes there's nothing positive left to say. In any case, it's important to have conversations about what's right with the couple instead of what's wrong with them. We do that by inviting the couple to talk about their best qualities and their desired future, even when couples find the discussion challenging. Consider this example from the session with Michelle and Stephanie:

Therapist: What would be different about the look in her eyes?

Michelle: She would not be sad.

Therapist: What would she be instead of being sad?

Michelle: Happy. She has a different look in her eyes when she is happy.

In Michelle's first answer, she simply used the absence of the problem as her descriptor—she couldn't come up with a positive way to describe the look in Stephanie's eyes. That's not enough for our solution-building purposes, so Michelle was invited to describe what Stephanie would be *instead* of sad, and it evoked a positive response.

Suppose is another effective word to use in inviting couples into solution-building conversations.

Therapist: *Suppose* by some chance you woke up tomorrow and that in-love feeling you have been describing to me, that glow was back. How would you notice it? If it just happened overnight somehow, what would be your very first clue?

Michelle: I wouldn't wake up crying.

Therapist: What would you be doing instead?

Michelle: I would be smiling and happy—hugs and kisses.

By starting a question with *suppose*, I was inviting Michelle to imagine something that had not happened yet—and she accepted the invitation, steering the conversation toward a description of the preferred future.

SELECTING WHICH PARTNER TO QUESTION

Deciding which partner to question at a particular moment in the session is an important skill for a couple's counselor. If the questioning isn't evenhanded, one partner may feel that he or she is not being heard, or that the therapist is siding with the other partner against them. Recall the idea that I call "solution-focused tennis," the process of asking questions to two people in turns. It's a way of ensuring that both partners have their say, and it keeps the conversation moving only in a direction that *both* partners approve of. The therapist must elicit responses from each partner to ensure equal contributions to the therapeutic process. In my conversation with Michelle and Stephanie, the back-and-forth of questions and answers resulted in a nearly equal distribution of responses from each partner. That didn't happen by chance. Each question was purposefully addressed to each partner in turns.

Solution building is a process of co-constructing a conversation between the couple and the therapist, and all three must take their turn in the conversation. No one can be allowed to dominate the conversation. This may mean that at times the therapist will have to interrupt one of the partners to ensure that the other can make a contribution.

THIRD-PERSON QUESTIONS

It sometimes happens that individuals will seek relationship therapy without their partners. In such cases, the therapist can use third-person questions to bring the absent partner into the conversation. *What would your husband notice this week if things got better, even though he's not here to tell us?* Such questions can lead to details that often prove nearly as helpful as first-person responses.

Third-person questions are also a powerful way to bring a couple's entire support system into the session. *How would your children notice that something was better? What would the people at work begin to see when your relationship is back to being it's very best? How would your dog react to having his best friend back in a happy relationship?* Questions like these can bring new points of view into a conversation and uncover details that can lead to change.

ASKING QUESTIONS WITH DIFFICULT COUPLES

In SFT, there are no difficult couples—period! The therapist must trust and believe in every couple and ask questions that they will find helpful. If a therapist allows himself or herself to see a couple as difficult, their ability to help them will be significantly impaired. If a couple doesn't find a therapist's questions helpful, the couple isn't being resistant—the therapist is asking the wrong questions. If a couple doesn't accept a therapist's suggested change, he or she isn't being difficult—the therapist is out of bounds (Lipchik, 2002). In solution building, the therapist isn't looking for ways a couple should change, but for the partners' talents, accomplishments, and dreams for the future.

USING PRESUMPTIVE LANGUAGE IN QUESTION DEVELOPMENT

Presumptive language is very important in developing solution-building questions. In the book, *Words Were Originally Magic* (1994), Steve de Shazer points out that therapy is nothing more than an exchange of words between people and that the words used greatly affect the conversation. Words are the tools we use to interact with our world, and the words we use can lead us toward or away from a desired change. In posing questions that use words like *when* and not *if*, or phrases like *suppose it happened* instead of *what if it happened*, couples are being asked to describe their world using unrealistic terms. The thinking that goes into answering a presumptive question is very different from the thinking needed to answer a merely hypothetical one.

Presumptive language also serves another useful purpose. It communicates the therapist's belief in a couple's ability to improve their relationship. Often this presumption alone helps couples to make positive changes in their relationship.

Solution-building questions have to be carefully constructed to optimize their helpfulness. Clinicians cannot know whether questions will be helpful until they're answered, but we always must craft them to communicate the therapist's underlying belief in the couple's abilities.

THE QUESTIONS

I thought it would be helpful to include a list of questions that can be used in the various steps of an SF conversation with couples. This is not *the* list of SF questions, it's simply a list of questions—drawn from a variety of sources—that I've found helpful over the years.

Step 1: Establishing a Direction

What are your best hopes from this meeting?

How are you hoping that being here will make a difference in your relationship?

What are your very best hopes?

What are your spouse's best hopes from this meeting?

What would be happening instead?

How would you notice that was happening?

How would you notice that being here was useful?

How would your spouse notice that being here was useful for you?

What needs to happen here, so that the two of you would view this as useful and not a waste of time?

After successful therapy, how would you like your relationship to be different?

Notice that all of the questions focus on what the relationship will look like after the therapy. From the beginning, solution building begins with the end in mind. Questions such as, "How can I help you?," "What brings you here today?," or "What would you like to talk about?," aren't appropriate questions because they invite a problem description instead of a description of the preferred future.

Step 2: Connecting With the Couple

How did you meet?

Where are you from?

Do you have children?

What do you do for a living?

Where do you go to school?

What do you do for fun?

When the relationship was at its best, what did you do for fun?

What is your partner's best quality?

What is it about your spouse that helped you fall in love?

How long did it take for the two of you to realize that there was a future in your relationship?

What were the signs at the very beginning that your partner was developing a romantic interest in you?

What do you enjoy most about the life the two of you have created together?

Who will be most affected when your relationship is once again at its best?

Have your children ever known the two of you when you were at your best?

Do any of your children display your or your partner's best qualities? How do they do this?

Now that I have gotten to know the two of you a bit better, do you have questions for me? Is there anything about me that you're curious about?

The questions aren't just about the couple—they're about the couple's strengths and best qualities. They also introduce members of the couple's support system (work, family, etc.) into the equation, so that those people can later be included in the solution-building process through third-person questions.

Step 3: Honeymoon Talk

When you were beginning this relationship, what steps did you take to ensure your partner was aware of your interest?

From the moment you first met to the happiest time in your relationship, what role did each of you play in that growth?

What skills do you each possess that led to such growth?

What traits did you rely upon to let the other person know you were capable of making him or her happy?

How did you show your partner that you would be a good match for them as the relationship was growing?

What did you notice about your partner that let you know that you'd done a good thing by entering into this relationship?

What is currently happening that gives you the idea that the traits that helped this relationship in the past are still present?

If somehow we had a videotape of one of your early dates, what would viewers see that would tell them you were in love?

What else?

What else?

What else?

The common theme here is digging for details of the couple's happy past, how they created it, and what skills they drew on in doing so. Couples often see their relationship as a random act rather than a deliberate creation. By asking these types of questions, the couple begins to realize that they played a role in their happy past—and could play a role in a happy future.

Step 4: The Preferred Future

Suppose, while you were asleep tonight, a miracle happened and returned your relationship to its very best state. What would you notice when you first wake up?

What would your partner notice?

What would be the very first smallest hint that something was different?

Suppose you wake up tomorrow and you were once again using your best skills to rebuild your relationship in a way that was right for you and your partner. What would be different?

What would those differences look like?

How would you let your spouse know to expect those differences from you?

Suppose tonight, while the two of you are sleeping, your relationship returned to the happiness that you experienced before you had children. What differences would your children notice?

If you showed up to work on the day this miracle happened, what differences would your co-workers notice about you?

What would your partner do to let you know the miracle had happened to him or her as well?

What difference would this make for you?

What difference would this make for your partner?

What else?

What else?

What else?

The questions here are crafted to create a picture of the preferred future and to fill it with as many details as possible. The richer and more specific preferred future becomes, the more meaningful it will be, and the more likely the couple will work toward it.

Step 5: Scaling

On a scale of zero to ten, if ten is the day your relationship is back at its best and zero is the day when you are as far away from that as possible, then where are you today?

Where were the two of you on the scale the day you decided to seek help from a therapist?

Because no one is perfect and no one can be a ten all the time, where would you like to be on the scale at the end of successful therapy?

How would you notice if you moved up one point?

How would you notice if your partner moved up one point?

In scaling, the task is to use the couple's worldview to measure their movement toward the preferred future, so it's important that the questions use the couple's own words to define points on the scale and not the therapist's words.

Step 6: Wrapping Up

Would you be willing to let your best traits play a bigger role in your relationship during the next days and weeks and to notice what that does to your ranking on the scale?

This week, could you please look for all the clues that this session was useful to you and notice what that does to your ranking on the scale?

This week, pick 1 hour a day and act as if the miracle has happened. I would ask you to notice how your children respond to seeing the two of you using your best traits toward one another.

These are just a few examples that demonstrate how the couple's language can be used to make suggestions. I don't always make suggestions, but when I do, they always come from the couple's own words and worldview.

MOVING FROM STEP TO STEP

In moving the conversation from one step to the next, time is the major consideration. How many minutes will you have for each step? There's no fixed answer. A typical therapy session lasts about an hour, and all the steps have to be completed within that timeframe. So although it's the therapist's job to keep to the schedule, the goal of the exercise is to amass as many useful details as possible. If a couple proves to be especially good at honeymoon talk, for example, don't be too quick to move on. You can make up for the lost time later, but a helpful detail that goes unspoken may be lost forever.

SUMMARY

It's important for the therapist to be aware of what stage of the session they are in at all times, because the sequence of the questions matters greatly. In SFT, the next question is always built on the answer that came before it. Asking unrelated questions leads nowhere. Chris Iveson (personal communication, 2009) thinks of the stages of an SF session as separate rooms—and the questions being asked must be relevant to the room the therapist is currently in. The goal is to build a conversation that moves from a couple's personal strengths to their past successes and their desired future, and the most successful conversations are the ones that start at the beginning.

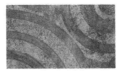

Final Thoughts

"Truth is what works."

—WILLIAM JAMES

I'd like to leave readers with a reminder that this book is composed largely of examples of the way I practice solution-focused therapy (SFT) with couples. My hope is not that readers will try to do things the way I do them, but rather that they will gain a practical understanding of the mechanics of SFT that might be useful in their own practices.

The other point I'd like to reiterate—a central premise of SFT—is the simple idea of hope. Client after client has proven to me that this form of therapy is effective.

In my early days, working with the children and families referred to my agency by the local drug court—clients who many therapists would consider difficult—I saw the power of SFT firsthand. My clients reported to me and other members of the treatment team that my conversations were helping them. Although many of my co-workers believed that SFT was not an "evidence-based" methodology—despite six positive evaluation studies in the mid-1990s and more than 50 follow-up studies in the years since (Macdonald, 2007)—all the evidence I needed was coming from my clients themselves. A judge in the drug program once called my supervisor to ask what I was doing differently than the other therapists at the agency. My families were graduating in the minimum 9-month period, whereas many of the families of my fellow clinicians were graduating in the maximum 18-month period, or failing to graduate at all. That was all the evidence I needed.

The clients at my next place of employment further solidified my belief in SFT, and it was there that I fell in love with couples therapy. Couple after couple was responding positively to the questions I was asking. Relationships were being renewed. Marriages were rebounding. Families were coming together again. The results were undeniable, but perhaps the most concrete evidence that I was making a difference came in the form of a Christmas card from the very first couple I'd seen. Once on the brink of divorce, the couple had stayed together and rebuilt a happy life for themselves, and the card they sent me included a family photograph and a note of thanks.

I still have that card in my office. I keep it with dozens of other cards and mementos I've received from other clients over the years on what I call the shelf of hope.

What follows are a few of my favorite things on that shelf.

THE PHOTOGRAPH

Steve and Mary sought counseling because their oldest son was having trouble in school. He'd been suspended a number of times and had recently been arrested for marijuana possession. When questioned by his parents, the son blamed his troubles on them—he couldn't take their constant fighting. Steve and Mary knew that they were having problems, of course, but they hadn't realized the impact it was having on their son. He was a junior in high school and had been a successful student and athlete in the previous years. The troubles had began at about the time Steve was laid off from his job.

In my very first session with the couple, I asked them, "If the miracle [a return to your happiest times as a couple] continued for some time after therapy, how would you know it?" Both Steve and Mary said the answer would come from their son—they would notice his behavior returning to what it had been when he was a standout student and athlete. Over the course of four sessions with them, Steve and Mary rediscovered the love in their relationship and were able to make enough significant changes in their lives that they felt they could discontinue therapy.

I didn't hear from Steve and Mary again for year and a half—when they sent me their son's high school graduation photo. They'd written, "Thank you, he made it!" across the back.

THE INVITATION

When I first met Dale and Laura, I couldn't figure out what they saw in each other—and they couldn't tell me. They spent all of their first two sessions arguing with each other. All I could figure out is that they wanted to rebuild their relationship, so that they could once again consider marriage. Dale and Laura were an older couple, and this would be a first marriage for both them. They reported that they argued regularly and that the arguments were often ugly and hurtful, and I had no doubt about it, I'd seen it with my own eyes. Both partners were unwilling to commit to marriage unless the situation could be turned around.

In the third session, I was finally able to ask the miracle question. "Suppose you woke up tomorrow and your relationship was back on track toward marriage how would you notice the change?" As the details came out, it was clear that their relationship was beginning to change just in the course of the conversation itself. The changes persisted between sessions—Dale and Laura bought a cat together, they decided which of their homes they'd live in, they agreed in principle how they would handle their money, and the arguing ended. Six months after their last session, Dale and Laura called to schedule another appointment. They simply wanted to share with me how much their relationship had improved and to deliver an invitation to their upcoming wedding.

THE EMAIL

The story of Joe and Jennifer is one of the more touching I've experienced in my years as a therapist. Jennifer first came to see me after she discovered that Joe was having an affair with a co-worker. She was understandably hurt by this but nonetheless wanted her relationship to continue. She thought that Joe was upset with her because she wanted another child and he didn't.

I saw Jennifer twice before Joe agreed to accompany her. In our first session together, it was clear that Joe was disappointed in himself for having the affair, and he too wanted to save his relationship with his wife. On the subject of a second child, Joe said his only concern was for Jennifer's health. There had been serious complications with her first pregnancy and he was worried about a second.

As we discussed their preferred future, both partners talked about rebuilding trust and possibility of a second child. As we talked, the discussion became more positive and future oriented—less about what had gone wrong and more about what their future would look like. I'd met with Joe and Jennifer three times as a couple when they learned that Joe was being transferred and they'd be moving to another state. At that point, their relationship was improving, but no decision about a baby had been reached.

I had to wait more than a year for this story's punch line to arrive by email. Joe and Jennifer sent me a sonogram of their twins! Mother and babies were doing fine.

CONCLUSION

Stories like these remind me how powerful it can be to shift the therapeutic emphasis from a problem story to a discussion of the preferred future. I understand and accept that many practitioners will continue to explore the underlying causes of the problems people experience in their lives, and I have no doubt that such explorations can be useful and valuable. But so long as I continue to witness the kinds of transformations I've recounted here, I will continue exploring the best in individuals and couples and help them put their problems—whatever they might be—behind them.

References

Connie, E., & Metcalf, L. (2009). *The art of solution focused therapy*. New York, NY: Springer.

Corey, G. (2001). *Theory and practice of counseling and psychotherapy* (6th ed.). Belmont, CA: Wadsworth Press.

De Jong, P., & Kim Berg, I. (2008). *Interviewing or solutions* (3rd ed.). Belmont, CA: Thomson Brooks/Cole.

De Shazer, S. (1985). *Keys to solution in brief in brief therapy*. New York, NY: W.W. Norton & Company.

De Shazer, S. (1988). *Clues: Investigating solutions in brief therapy*. New York, NY: W.W. Norton & Company.

De Shazer, S. (1994). *Words were originally magic*. New York, NY: W.W. Norton & Company.

De Shazer, S., Dolan, Y., Korman, H., Trepper, T., McCollum, E., & Kim Berg, I. (2007). *More than miracles: The state of the art of solution-focused brief therapy*. Binghamton, NY: The Haworth Press.

George, E., Iveson, C., & Ratner, H. (2006). *Problem to solution: Brief therapy with individuals and families* (2nd ed.). London, England: Brief Therapy Press.

George, E., Iveson, C., & Ratner, H. (2011). *Briefer: A solution focused manual*. London, England: BRIEF Therapy Press.

Haley, J. (1984). *Ordeal therapy*. San Francisco, CA: Josey Bass.

Haley, J. (1993). *Uncommon therapy: The psychiatric techniques of Milton H. Erickson MD*. New York, NY: W.W. Norton & Company.

Lipchik, E. (2002). *Beyond technique in solution focused therapy: Working with emotions and the therapeutic relationship*. New York, NY: The Guilford Press.

Macdonald, A. (2007). *Solution-focused therapy: Theory, research & practice*. London, England: Sage Publications.

Minuchin, S. (1974). *Families and family therapy.* Cambridge, MA: Harvard University Press.

Walter, J., & Peller, J. (1992). *Becoming solution focused in brief therapy.* New York, NY: Taylor and Francis Group.

Zeig, J., & Gilligan, S. (Eds.). (1990). *Brief therapy: Myths, methods, and metaphors.* New York, NY: Bruner/Mazel.

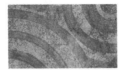

Index